371.20071
MUR
Murphy, Joseph
Preparing school leader~ ~fining
a research and actio~   ~

Preparing
School Leaders

Defining a Research and
Action Agenda

Joseph Murphy

Published in partnership with the
University Council for Educational Administration
and the Stanford Educational Leadership Institute

Rowman & Littlefield Education
Lanham, Maryland • Toronto • Oxford
2006

JOLIET JUNIOR COLLEGE
JOLIET, IL 60431

Published in partnership with the
University Council for Education Administration
and the Stanford Educational Leadership Institute

Published in the United States of America
by Rowman & Littlefield Education
A Division of Rowman & Littlefield Publishers, Inc.
A wholly owned subsidiary of The Rowman & Littlefield Publishing Group, Inc.
4501 Forbes Boulevard, Suite 200, Lanham, Maryland 20706
www.rowmaneducation.com

PO Box 317
Oxford
OX2 9RU, UK

Copyright © 2006 by Joseph Murphy

All rights reserved. No part of this publication may be reproduced,
stored in a retrieval system, or transmitted in any form or by any
means, electronic, mechanical, photocopying, recording, or otherwise,
without the prior permission of the publisher.

British Library Cataloguing in Publication Information Available

Library of Congress Cataloging-in-Publication Data
Preparing school leaders : defining a research and action agenda /
[edited by] Joseph Murphy.
    p. cm.
  "Published in partnership with the University Council for Education
Administration and the Stanford Educational Leadership Institute."
  Includes bibliographical references and index.
  ISBN-13: 978-1-57886-427-0 (hardcover : alk. paper)
  ISBN-13: 978-1-57886-428-7 (pbk. : alk. paper)
  ISBN-10: 1-57886-427-5 (hardcover : alk. paper)
  ISBN-10: 1-57886-428-3 (pbk. : alk. paper)
  1. Educational leadership–United States. 2. School administrators–United States.
3. School management and organization–United States. I. Murphy, Joseph.
LB2805.P765 2006
371.20071'1–dc22   2005037231

⊚™ The paper used in this publication meets the minimum requirements of
American National Standard for Information Sciences—Permanence of
Paper for Printed Library Materials, ANSI/NISO Z39.48-1992.
Manufactured in the United States of America.

371.2007/
MUR

Contents

JOLIET JUNIOR COLLEGE
JOLIET, IL 60431

Dedication

To James "Big Jim" Murphy

Acknowledgments

The paper from which this book was developed was supported by the Stanford Grant on Innovative Principal Training Programs. The support of the Wallace Foundation and the University Council for Educational Administration in developing and publishing this book is gratefully acknowledged.

Foreword

Educational leadership preparation programs need a wake-up call, and Joseph Murphy provides one! His timely book, *Preparing School Leaders: Defining a Research and Action Agenda*, addresses a subject that warrants scrutiny by scholars and practitioners alike. Even former skeptics now concur that administrators play a key role in determining school success, but the preparation of such leaders has been overlooked in education reform efforts. Murphy argues persuasively that reconceptualizing school leadership and leadership preparation is an essential step in achieving collaborative and continuous school improvement.

To provide a context for his clarion call for research and action regarding leadership preparation, Murphy chronicles the history of how school administrators have been trained, and he shows that research in this arena has been woefully inadequate. He urges researchers to conduct comprehensive studies of the status of leadership preparation at regular intervals, similar to those published on the professoriate, and he notes that the last comprehensive study of the structure and content of preparation programs was more than a quarter century ago. Murphy also calls for empirical investigations to replace the testimonials about various innovations adopted over the past few decades, such as the use of problem-based learning, student cohorts, and expanded internships. In short, have these changes in preparation programs produced more successful school leaders who do a better job of creating educationally effective learning environments?

Murphy makes special pleas for the field to give more attention to education outcomes and to address the serious research void pertaining to the key relationships between leadership and teaching and learning.

The picture Murphy paints regarding research on leadership preparation is not without some promising signs. He is encouraged by the University Council for Educational Administration conventions that have focused in part on preparation program reform and given legitimacy to inquiry in this arena. Also, the American Educational Research Association special interest group on Teaching in Educational Administration similarly has increased the visibility and credibility of efforts to strengthen preparation programs. Given these and other developments, Murphy observes that the amount of research on preparation programs has increased in the past 15 years, but still only about one tenth of the articles in leading educational leadership journals focus on administrator preservice training and less than half of these entail empirical studies.

Although scholarship is starting to expand beyond perceptions of graduates and faculty, there are still no studies assessing the skills and knowledge gained in preparation programs or changes in student performance in the schools graduates lead. Moreover, studies of programs considered highly effective are nearly nonexistent. Murphy calls for the practice and academic arms of the profession to come together to identify a small number of significant issues that can be addressed collectively to produce meaningful results. And he urges the field to provide a forum for such research to be disseminated at national meetings of practitioner and research organizations.

Among this book's numerous strengths is its emphasis on the environment in which the preparation of school leaders occurs. Murphy notes that research on the context of leadership training has been lacking, which is especially troubling when external conditions are rapidly changing. Given the global economy, technological advances that have revolutionized communication and even changed the concept of "school," the shift from government control toward market control of education, and other societal developments, Murphy argues that research on the context of leadership preparation is sorely needed.

He also explores the sensitive topic of alternatives to university preparation of school leaders, providing useful descriptions of private models, school district programs, and activities of professional associations in this regard. These new preparation models are likely to expand, so instead of universities being threatened, Murphy calls for them to explore how various preparation configurations can produce better school leaders and ultimately improve our nation's schools. He builds a case for collaboration and partnerships among school personnel, universities, for-profit groups, and professional organizations. He urges the field to conduct empirical studies on these alternatives, so informed decisions can be made regarding the best strategies to prepare school leaders for the future.

Joseph Murphy makes us think seriously about the condition of leadership preparation and steps that can be taken to enhance its quality. Because of the significant internal and external challenges, more of the same is not an option and complacency is intolerable. Instead of simply lamenting what *is*, Murphy moves us to what *can be*. He outlines bold strategies to make research on leadership preparation more meaningful and visible. For this, we are in his debt. Faculty members, policymakers, and practitioners must read this monograph and, more importantly, respond in thoughtful and purposeful ways.

Martha McCarthy
Chancellor's Professor, Indiana University

1

Setting the Stage

To be prepared to provide effective leadership—leadership that leads to improvement in student performance—preparation and professional development must be redesigned. (Grogan & Andrews, 2002, p. 250)

The message here is threefold. First, while it is imperative that we address problems plaguing current programs, it is insufficient to build a new vision for educational administration primarily as a foil to existing deficiencies. Second, we are unlikely to be successful in constructing better programs unless we attend to our history, or, in the words of Cubberly (cited in Culbertson, 1988), the "proper means for reconstructing our social institutions are best suggested by a careful accumulation and analysis of our institutional experience" (p. 9). Third, we are likely to develop more effective models of preparation only if we ground our program conceptions in visions of society, education, learning, and leadership for schooling in the twenty-first century as well as in the values and evidence that define the paths to those visions. (Murphy, 1993, p. 2)

SETTING THE STAGE

For much of the past quarter century, academics and practitioners have been engaged in an unbroken quest to understand the school improvement algorithm (Murphy & Adams, 1998; Teddlie & Reynolds, 2000). That is, there have been ongoing efforts, sometimes systematic and often ad hoc,

to isolate the variables in the school performance equation and to understand how they work, both as individual components and as parts of
the system of schooling. Across this time, investigators have paid special
attention to conditions in schools that help explain the dramatic over-
representation of selected groups of youngsters in the underperforming
and failing categories of the school success taxonomy (Snow, Burns, &
Griffin, 1998).

From this work, we have discovered a good deal about how schools
work to promote, or fail to promote, student achievement. For example,
we know that quality instruction (Anderson, Hiebert, Scott, & Wilkinson,
1985; Ferguson & Ladd, 1996) and opportunity to learn (time, content,
and success rate) (Cooley & Leinhardt, 1980; Denham & Lieberman,
1980) explain a good deal of student performance. In a similar vein, we
have learned that robust connections between home and school focusing
on academic mission (Chall, Jacobs, & Baldwin, 1990; Cotton & Savard,
1980; Rowe, 1995) and thoughtful professional development in the context of communities of practice (Elmore, 1996; Little & McLaughlin,
1993, 1993b; Stigler & Hiebert, 1999) are important links in the school
improvement chain.

Research throughout the past quarter century in education has also
underscored leadership as a crucial theme in the school improvement
narrative (Murphy, 1988, 1990b; Murphy & Datnow, 2003; Wellisch,
MacQueen, Carriere, & Duck, 1978). Indeed, evidence from nearly
every realm of investigation beginning with effective schools studies
(Hallinger, 1981; Murphy, Hallinger, & Mesa, 1985; Purkey & Smith,
1983) through the most recent work on comprehensive school reform
(Copland, 2003; Smylie, Wenzel, & Fendt, 2003) confirms leadership as
an explanatory variable in schools where all students meet ambitious
achievement targets.

As is often the case, enhanced recognition has been accompanied by increased scrutiny (Murphy, 1990b). And, not unexpectedly, the spotlight
has revealed both positive attributes and flaws in how we think about and
practice leadership in schools. For example, at the same time that some re-
searches were uncovering the importance of learning-centered work for
principals and superintendents (see Murphy, 1990a; Murphy & Hallinger,
1986), other analysts were documenting that leadership in schools, as
commonly enacted, had little to do with education—that the calculus of

leadership in schools was a composite of management, politics, and organization (Bates, 1984; Evans, 1991).

As understanding of leadership in the work of school reform began to deepen, more and more attention was directed to the qualifications of the women and men who occupy leadership roles in schools. Consequently, considerable interest was devoted to the preparation of those leaders. And, as I discuss in some detail, analyses of the preparation function exposed a profession in need of major improvements—in how it recruited and selected students, in the content it stressed, in the ways it provided learning opportunities, in the procedures used to assess student learning, and in the strategies engaged to evaluate its own performance.

My analysis in this book is devoted to this last link in the discussion, that is, to the education of school leaders. In chapter 2, I provide a brief historical treatment of the education of school leaders. In chapters 3 through 6, I unpack the forces shaping the reconceptualization of preservice training programs. I examine broader forces in play, such as changes in our understanding of school organizations, and review major problems with the current system. I outline the most important markers in the struggle to overhaul preparation programs and tease out the major trends that define that reform work. Based on these analyses, in chapter 7 and 8, I craft an agenda for strengthening research and practice on the preparation function in school leadership. I turn now to the historical context that helps give meaning to the material in the following chapters.

2

A Historical Note on Preparation

PREPARING SCHOOL ADMINISTRATORS, 1900–1946

Although school administrators were in evidence before the turn of the century, little was written on the topic of school leadership "and formal preparation programs for school administrators had not yet developed" (Gregg, 1960, p. 20). Prior to 1900, character (Tyack & Hansot, 1982) and ideology (Glass, 1986) were important characteristics of school leaders. Administrators of this era have been characterized as philosopher educators (Callahan & Button, 1964) and as teachers of teachers (Button, 1966).

The 20th century ushered in the beginning of the prescriptive era in school administration (Campbell, Fleming, Newell, & Bennion, 1987), a nearly 50-year period of expansion in training programs for school leaders. In 1900, no institutions were offering systematic study in the area of school management. By the end of World War II, 125 institutions were actively engaged in preparing school administrators (Silver, 1982). A first generation of educational administration professors—men like Cubberly, Strayer, and Mort—were actively engaged in laying the foundations of the field and in training a second generation of professors to take their place. Many states were requiring formal course work in educational leadership for administrative positions and were certifying graduates of preparation programs for employment (Moore, 1964). As these elements of the profession began to find acceptance, more and more principals and superintendents embarked on their careers with university training in school administration.

This shift from an era of teaching, ideology, character, and philosophy to one of prescription represents the first era of ferment in school administration—one marked by a number of trends that I see repeated during both the second (1947–1957) and third (1986–2000) periods of ferment in the profession (see Figure 1). All three periods witnessed much critical analysis about the health of educational administration in general and the status of preparation programs in particular. There was considerable muckraking literature about the way administrators were managing schools (Cooper & Boyd, 1987). In addition, new views of leadership that reflected dominant social and cultural forces were held up as desirable alternatives for training educational administrators (Callahan, 1962; Murphy, 1992).

Information on the preparation of school leaders following the first era of ferment is limited and uneven, gaining in clarity as we approach World War II. Faculty members of this era were drawn almost exclusively from the superintendency. They carried heavy teaching loads and showed little proclivity for research. A similar homogeneity characterized students of this period. Most were white males holding full-time positions as school administrators while attending school on a part-time basis (Campbell et al., 1987). Some trained for the professoriate, most for the superintendency (Silver, 1982).

The education received by superintendents and principals was largely undifferentiated from that of teachers until the onslaught and widespread acceptance of the scientific management movement throughout the

1820–1900 Ideological Era

First Era of Ferment (1900–1915)

1900–1946 Prescriptive Era

Second Era of Ferment (1947–1957)

1947–1985 Scientific Era

Third Era of Ferment (1986–2000)

1986? Dialectic Era

Figure 1. The Eras of Ferment in School Administration

corporate world between 1910 and 1915. For the next 20 years, business was to exert considerable influence over preparation programs for school administrators. During this time, "preservice education for school executives tended to stress: the technical and mechanical aspects of administration" (Gregg, 1969, p. 994), "specific and immediate tasks" (Callahan & Button, 1964, p. 87), and the practical aspects of the job (Newlon, 1934). The objective was to train students to understand the job of administration as it was and to perform successfully in the roles they undertook—what Campbell and his colleagues (1987) label preparation for the role—as opposed to studying what might need to be done differently and preparing for roles as change agents, that is, preparing the person.

While the Great Depression and World War II saw the incorporation of new material into training programs—"human relations in cooperative educational activities" (Gregg, 1969, p. 994), social foundations, and the human factor in general—by the end of the prescriptive era preparation was still highly technical in nature. Almost no attention was given to the theoretical underpinnings of the work of school leaders.

The scholarship that informed course content throughout this era was little more than "naked empiricism" (Griffiths, 1965, p. 34; Halpin, 1957, p. 197) or "factualism" (Griffiths, 1959, p. 9), resulting in the development of "fuzzy concepts" (Griffiths, 1988b, p. 29), "inadequately field-tested principles" (Crowson & McPherson, 1987, p. 47), and a mere "encyclopedia of facts" (Griffiths, 1959, p. 9) that lacked "the power of unifying interpretive theories" (Tyack & Cummings, 1977, p. 62; Goldhammer, 1983). The knowledge base was comprised of "folklore, testimonials of reputedly successful administrators, . . . the speculation of college professors" (Griffiths, 1959, p. v), "personal success stories and lively anecdotes" (Marland, 1960, p. 25), "personal accounts or 'war stories,' and prescriptions offered by experienced practitioners" (Silver, 1982, p. 51), "experiences of practicing administrators as they managed the various problem areas of school administration" (Gregg, 1969, p. 996), "maxims, exhortations, and several innocuous variations on the theme of the Golden Rule" (Halpin, 1960, p. 4), and "preachments to administrators about ways in which they should perform" (Goldhammer, 1983, p. 250; cited in Murphy, 1992, pp. 31–32).

PREPARING SCHOOL ADMINISTRATORS, 1947–1985

Beginning in the late 1940s and continuing throughout the 1950s and 1960s, prescriptions drawn from practice came to be overshadowed in preparation programs by theoretical and conceptual material drawn from the various social sciences. Like the prescriptive era before it, the scientific era, in its emergence, drew support because of its harsh attacks on the status quo in the area of administrative training, its critical analyses of the performance of existing school leaders, and its lure of an alternative vision—science, in this case—that held forth the promise of dramatically improving the education available to prospective school leaders.

At the onset of the scientific era, considerable criticism was leveled against the naked empiricism, personal success stories, and maxims or untested principles that constituted the knowledge base of educational administration at the time. It was also argued by many that the explicit values framework of the latter half of the prescriptive era—the human relations era—was inappropriate in a scientific world. In the first period of ferment in school leadership (1900–1915), practicing administrators were chastised for their lack of grounding in the management principles of the corporate world, especially those developed by Frederick Taylor and his peers. In this second era of ferment (1947–1957), they came under attack for their unscientific, nontheoretical approach to administration (McCarthy, 1999). Throughout this second era of ferment, training institutions were being exhorted to develop better preparation programs "to protect the public against ill-prepared or indifferent practitioners" (Goldhammer, 1983, p. 253). In addition, as has been the case throughout the history of school management, professors began to reweave the fabric of preparation programs to mirror the high-status professions in the larger society, thereby creating an alternative vision of the role of school administrators (Button, 1966; Callahan, 1962; Callahan & Button, 1964). Because scientists, not business people, held center stage at this time (Halpin, 1960), a quest for a science of school administration was undertaken (Culbertson, 1965, 1988; Greenfield, 1988; Griffiths, 1988b).

This second period of ferment in school administration was characterized by considerable enthusiasm, activity, growth, and dramatic changes in the structure and content of training programs (Crowson & McPherson, 1987; Willower, 1983; Wynn, 1957). It was a period that many believed would lead to the full professionalization of school administration (Far-quhar, 1977; Goldhammer, 1983).

Four major events mark the second era of ferment. The first of these was the formation of the National Conference of Professors of Educational Administration (NCPEA) in 1947. By linking professors throughout the country for the first time, the NCPEA exercised considerable influence over emerging conceptions of the profession and over school administration training programs (Campbell et al., 1987; Gregg, 1960). The second defining event in the transition from the prescriptive to the scientific era was the creation of the Cooperative Project in Educational Administration (CPEA)—a consortium of eight universities funded by the Kellogg Foundation, whose primary purpose was to institute changes in preparation programs. Continuing initiatives charted at earlier NCPEA meetings, especially the "benchmark" 1954 gathering in Denver (Getzels, 1977, p. 8), the CPEA encouraged a multidisciplinary approach to analyses of administration and to the education of school leaders. As Gregg concluded in his 1969 review, the CPEA had a profound influence on preparation programs and on the practice of school administration. The establishment of the Committee for the Advancement of School Administration (CASA) in 1955 and of the University Council for Educational Administration (UCEA) in 1956 represent the final milestones that helped shape evolving conceptions of school administration during the second era of ferment (Forsyth, 1999; Griffiths, 1959; Moore, 1964). The CASA's most important work focused on the development of professional standards of performance. The UCEA's influence has been more pervasive (Forsyth, 1999; Willower, 1983). Throughout the 1960s and 1970s, UCEA "became the dominant force in shaping the study and teaching of educational administration . . . [and] a major force in the advancement of preparation programs" (Campbell et al., 1987, pp. 182–183).

Under the pull of these forces, there was a considerable flurry of activity in preparation programs throughout the country during the scientific era, especially during the 1950s and 1960s. This was a period of rapid growth in educational administration. While in 1946, approximately 125 institutions were in the business of preparing school leaders, 40 years later, over 500 were involved (National Commission on Excellence in Educational Administration, 1987). The number of doctoral degrees doubled during each decade throughout this period (Farquhar, 1977). The size of the typical program—defined in terms of number of faculty—increased substantially during the heyday of the scientific era, doubling in size from 5 to 10 full-time faculty members (Farquhar, 1977) before falling back to its original size by the mid-1980s (McCarthy, Kuh, Newell, & Iacona, 1988).

The average faculty member in 1945 was most likely to be a generalist, drawn from the superintendency, and oriented primarily toward the practice dimensions of the profession. By the mid-1980s, that picture had changed considerably. The typical faculty member in educational administration at the end of the scientific era was likely to be a discipline-focused specialist with little or no practical experience, concerned primarily with the professorial (if not scholarly) aspects of the profession. While there was considerably more diversity among students in preparation programs in 1985 than in 1945 in terms of gender, and to a lesser extent race, there were still many commonalities. Most students continued to be drawn from the bottom quartile on national entrance exams, self-selected their programs, attended local institutions on a part-time basis, and exercised little control over their lives as students (Murphy, 1990b).

Consistent with the guiding vision of the scientific era, the predominant trend during this 40-year period was the infusion of content from the social sciences into preparation programs (McCarthy, 1999; Murphy, 1992). The infrastructure for this activity was the expansion of the conceptual and theoretical knowledge base of the profession through the development of a science of administration. This was a movement intended "to produce a foundation of scientifically supported (hypothetico-deductive) knowledge in educational administration in place of the hortatory, seat-of-the-pants literature already in place" (Crowson & McPherson, 1987, pp. 47–48) and a trend "away from technique-oriented substance based upon practical experience and toward theory-oriented substance based on disciplines 'external' to education" (Culbertson & Farquhar, 1971, p. 9). The scientific movement led to a conception of educational administration as "an applied science within which theory and research are directly and linearly linked to professional practice [and in which] the former always determine the latter, and thus knowledge is superordinate to the principal

and designed to prescribe practice" (Sergiovanni, 1991, p. 4); the acceptance of a heavy reliance on social science content "as an indicator of a
high quality program" (Miklos, 1983, p. 160); "the borrowing and adopt-
ing of research techniques and instruments from the behavioral sciences"
(Culbertson, 1965, p. 7); and a multidisciplinary (if not interdisciplinary)
approach to preparation (Culbertson, 1963; Hodgkinson, 1975).

3

Preparing School Administrators, 1986; Change Forces

For the past 20 years, educational administration has been in the throes of a third era of ferment, one that appears to be accompanying the shift from a scientific to a postscientific or dialectic era in school administration. As was true in each of the proceeding two eras, this latest ferment is being fueled by devastating attacks on the state of preparation programs, critical analyses of practicing school administrators, and references to alternative visions of what programs should become. If anything, the rhetoric in this third period of ferment seems both more strident and more comprehensive than that found in earlier eras of reform (Hallinger & Murphy, 1991). The seriousness of the rhetoric has also increased.

> School administrators risk becoming an anachronism if their preparation programs in schools, colleges, and departments of education do not respond to calls for change in preparing them for professional leadership functions (American Association of Colleges for Teacher Education, 1998, p. 1). I am thoroughly and completely convinced that, unless a radical reform movement gets under way—and is successful—most of us in this room will live to see the end of educational administration as a profession. (Griffiths, 1988a, p. 1)
>
> Educational Administration as a field is at a delicately critical phase. In fact, there is a rumbling in the clouds above us—they are no longer merely on the horizon—which could in fact blow the whole field of Educational Administration apart, for both practitioners and the scholars in the field. (Beare, 1989, p. 3)

In chapter 4, I explore the forces that have fueled the movement to the current phase in the preparation of school administrators. Because I agree with McCarthy (1999) that "to fully understand . . . university programs that prepare school leaders it is necessary to explore the external forces that have helped shape them" (p. 119), I begin with a discussion of the changing environment of school administration—environmental forces associated with the evolution to a postindustrial, postmodern world and forces changing the nature of schooling of which school administration is a part. In chapter 5, I highlight change forces inside school leadership.

4

The Evolution to a Postindustrial World

THE CHANGING ECONOMIC FABRIC

It is almost a fundamental law that the economy is undergoing a significant metamorphosis as we begin the 21st century. There is widespread agreement that we have been and continue to be moving from an industrial to a postindustrial or informational economy. Key aspects of the new economy include the globalization of economic activity, the demise of the mass-production economy, a privileging of information technology, an increase in the skills required to be successful, and an emphasis on the service dimensions of the marketplace (Marshall & Tucker, 1992). It is also becoming clear to many analysts that with the arrival of the postindustrial society, "we are seeing the dissolution of the social structure associated with traditional industrialism" (Hood, 1994, p. 12). The ascent of the global economy has brought an emphasis on new markets, "a loosening of the constraints of the labor market" (Dahrendorf, 1995, p. 13–39), and a "break[ing] of the state monopoly on the delivery of human services so that private enterprise can expand" (Lewis, 1993, p. 84). Along with these have come increasing deinstitutionalization, deregulation, and privatization.

There is a growing belief that "free market economics provide the path to prosperous equilibrium" (Thayer, 1987, p. 168)—a belief in "the assumption that, left to itself, economic interaction between rationally self-interested individuals in the market will spontaneously yield broad prosperity, social harmony, and all other manner of public and private good"

(Himmelstein, 1983, p. 16). Supported by market theory and theories of the firm and by the public choice literature, there is a "new spirit of enterprise in the air" (Hardin, 1989, p. 16)—a renewed interest in "private market values" (Bailey, 1987, p. 141) , in the "virtues of private property" (Hirsch, 1991, p. 2), and in a "promarket trend" (President's Commission on Privatization, 1988, p. 237) in the larger society. A view of individuals as "economic free agents" (Murnane & Levy, 1996, p. 229) is finding widespread acceptance. While analysts are quick to point out the fallacy of this emerging belief in the infallibility of markets, there is little doubt that current alterations in the economic foundations of society are anchored firmly on a "belief in the superiority of free market forms of social organization over the forms of social organization of the Keynesian welfare state society" (Ian Taylor, cited in Martin, 1993, p. 48). As Starr (1991) notes, this expanding reliance on the market moves individuals in the direction of "exercis[ing] choice as consumers rather than as citizens" (p. 27). This evolution from government to markets has profound implications for education writ large and for emerging conceptions of schooling and for school leadership and the preparation of school leaders.

SHIFTING SOCIAL AND POLITICAL DYNAMICS

In the previous section, I addressed the changing economic substructures of a postindustrial state. In this section, I examine the shifting social and political foundations of the democratic welfare state that in turn act to help redefine the education industry and our understanding of school leadership. The political and social environment appears to be undergoing important changes. There has been a loosening of the bonds of democracy (Barber, 1984). Thus, according to a number of scholars, "our American democracy is faltering" (Elshtain, 1995, p. 1), with a concomitant "loss . . . to our ways of living and working together and to our view of the worth of the individual" (Tomlinson, 1986, p. 211). The infrastructure of civil society also has been impaired. Analysts discern fairly significant tears in the fabric known as "modern civil society" (Dahrendorf, 1995, p. 13–39). As a consequence of these basic shifts—the weakening of democracy and the deterioration of civil society, especially in conjunction with the ideological space that they share with economic fundamentalism—important sociopolitical trends have begun to emerge: (a) "a growing sense of personal insecurity" (Dahrendorf, 1995, p. 13–39), "unrest in the populace at large" (Liebman & Wuthnow, 1983, p. 3), and a less predictable "worldlife" (Hawley, 1995, pp. 741–742); (b) "the destruction of important features of community life" (Dahrendorf, 1995, p. 13–39); (c) shifts in the boundaries—both real and symbolic—between the state and alternative sociopolitical structures (Liebman, 1983a); and (d) an expanding belief that the enhancement of social justice through collective action, especially public action, is unlikely (Whitty, 1984). The composite picture of self-destruction has been labeled "The Disunity of America" by Dahrendorf (1995, p. 13–39) and characterized as "the weakening . . . of the world known as democratic civil society" by Elshtain (1995, p. 2). One strand of this evolving sociopolitical mosaic is plummeting public support for government (Cibulka, 1999). In many ways, Americans "have disengaged psychologically from politics and governance" (Putnam, 1995, p. 68): "The growth of cynicism about democratic government shifts America toward, not away from, a more generalized norm of disaffection" (Elshtain, 1995, p. 25). As Hawley (1995) chronicles, "Citizens are becoming increasingly alienated from government and politics. They do not trust public officials" (p. 741), and they are skeptical of the bureaucratic quagmire of professional control. A second pattern in the mosaic is defined by issues of poverty (Cibulka, 1999; Reyes, Wagstaff, & Fusarelli, 1999). Many analysts, for example, have detailed the "concept and the phenomenon of the underclass" (Dahrendorf, 1995, p. 13–39) or the "trend toward private wealth and public squalor" (Bauman, 1996, p. 627). According to Dahrendorf (1995), this economically grounded trend represents a new type of social exclusion—the "systematic divergence of the life chances for large social groups" (p. 13–39). He and others are quick to point out that this condition seriously undermines the health of society: "Poverty and unemployment threaten the very fabric of civil society. . . . Once these [work and a decent standard of living] are lost by a growing number of people, civil society goes with them" (pp. 13–39). Consistent with this description of diverging life chances is a body of findings on the declining social welfare of children and their families (Reyes et al., 1999). These data reveal a society populated increasingly by groups of citizens that historically have not fared well in this nation, especially ethnic minorities and citizens for whom English is a second language. Concomitantly, the percentage of youngsters affected by the ills of the world in which they live—for example, poverty,

unemployment, illiteracy, crime, drug addiction, malnutrition, poor physical
health—is increasing. According to Himmelstein (1983), society is best pic-
tured as "a web of shared values and integrating institutions that bind individuals together and restrain their otherwise selfish, destructive drives"
(p. 16). Some reviewers have observed a noticeable attenuation of these social bonds, what Elshtain (1995) describes as a "loss of civil society—a kind
of evacuation of civic spaces" (p. 5). The splintering of shared values and
the accompanying diminution in social cohesiveness have been discussed
by Dahrendorf (1995) and Mayberry (1991), among others. Few, however,
have devoted as much attention to the topic of changing patterns of civic engagement and political participation as Robert Putnam (1995). According to
Putnam, the "democratic disarray" (p. 77) that characterizes society and the
polity can be "linked to a broad and continuing erosion of civic engagement
that began a quarter-century ago" (p. 77). After examining citizen involvement across a wide array of areas (e.g., participation in politics, union membership, volunteerism in civic and fraternal organizations, participation in
organized religion), he drew the following conclusion:

> By almost every measure, Americans' direct engagement in politics and
> government has fallen steadily and sharply over the last generation, despite
> the fact that average levels of education—the best individual-level predic-
> tor of political participation—have risen sharply throughout this period.
> Every year over the last decade or two, millions more have withdrawn from
> the affairs of their communities. (p. 68)

Another piece of the story, related to the themes of declining social cohesion and political abstinence but even more difficult to ignore, is the issue
of "social breakdown and moral decay" (Himmelstein, 1983, p. 15), or
rents in the "sociomoral" (Liebman, 1983b, p. 229) tapestry of society. Of
particular concern is the perception that state actions have contributed to
the evolution of social mores that are undermining the adhesiveness that
has traditionally held society together—that "the welfare bureaucracy is
irreversibly opposed to the established social morality" (Gottfried, 1993,
p. 86). The ideological footings of the emerging sociopolitical infrastructure are only dimly visible at this time. The one piece of the foundation
that shines most brightly is what Tomlinson (1986) describes as the
"ascendancy of the theory of the social market" (p. 211)—a theory that is

anchored on the "supreme value [of] individual liberty" (p. 211). This emerging "high regard for personal autonomy, or liberty" (Gottfried, 1993, pp. xiv–xv) is both an honoring of individualization and a discrediting of collective action (Donahue, 1989; Katz, 1971). Social market theory suggests a "reduced role for government, greater consumer control, and a belief in efficiency and individuality over equity and community" (Bauman, 1996, p. 627). According to Whitty (1984), it includes the privileging of private over public delivery and "the restoration of decisions that have been made by professional experts over the last few decades to the individuals whose lives are involved" (p. 53). While critics of social market theory and glorified individualism foresee "a weakening of democratic participation [and] social cohesion" (Tomlinson, 1986, p. 211), advocates contend that "the individual pursuit of self interest is not a threat to the social bond, but its very basis" (Himmelstein, 1983, p. 16).

5

The Changing Nature of Schooling

As is the case with other organizations, schools are currently fighting to transform the way they think and act. From the collective effort of those who describe this change, a new vision of education quite unlike the "center of production" (Barth, 1986, p. 295) image that has shaped schooling throughout the industrial age is being portrayed. Embedded in this emerging view of tomorrow's schools are three central alterations: (a) at the institutional level, a rebalancing of the equation that adds more weight to market and citizen control while subtracting influence from government and professional actors; (b) at the managerial level, a change from a bureaucratic operational system to more communal views of schooling; and (c) at the technical level, a change from behavioral to social-constructivist views of learning and teaching. Each or these fundamental shifts leads to different ways of thinking about the profession of school administration and the education of school leaders (Louis & Murphy, 1994; Murphy & Louis, 1999).

REINVENTING GOVERNANCE

Most analysts of the institutional level of schooling—the interface of the school with its larger (generally immediate) environment—argue that the industrial approach to education led to a "cult of professionalism" (Sarason, 1994, p. 84) and to the "almost complete separation of schools from the community and, in turn, discouragement of local community involvement in decision making related to the administration of schools" (Burke, 1992, p. 33) and helped "marginalize parents as co-producers of their children's learning" (Consortium on Productivity in the Schools, 1995, p. 57). Critiques of extant governance systems center on two topics: (a) frustration with the government–professional monopoly and (b) critical analyses of the basic governance infrastructure—bureaucracy.

Most chroniclers of the changing governance structures in schools envision the demise of schooling as a sheltered government monopoly heavily controlled by professionals (Murphy, 1999c, 2000). As noted above, in its stead they forecast the emergence of a system of schooling driven by economic and political forces that substantially increase the saliency of market and democratic dynamics (see Murphy, 1996; Murphy, Gilmer, Weise, & Page, 1998). Embedded in this conception are a number of interesting dynamics. One of the key elements involves a recalibration of the locus of control based on what Ross (1988) describes as "a review and reconsideration of the division of existing responsibilities and functions" (p. 2) among levels of government. Originally called "democratic localism" (p. 305) by Katz (1971), it has more recently come to be known simply as localization or, more commonly, decentralization. However it is labeled, it represents a backlash against "the thorough triumph of a centralized and bureaucratic form of educational organization" (p. 305) and governance and an antidote for the feeling that "America has lost its way in education because America has disenfranchised individual local schools" (Guthrie, 1997, p. 34).

A second ideological foundation can best be thought of as a recasting of democracy, a replacement of representative governance with more populist conceptions, especially what Cronin (1989) describes as direct democracy. While I use the term more broadly than does Cronin, my conception shares with his a grounding in (a) the falling fortunes of representative democracy, (b) a "growing distrust of legislative bodies . . . [and] a growing suspicion that privileged interests exert far greater influence on the typical politician than does the common voter" (p. 4), and (c) recognition of the claims of its advocates that greater direct voice will produce important benefits for society—that it "could enrich citizenship and replace distrust of government with respect and healthy participation" (p. 48).

A third foundation encompasses a rebalancing of the governance equation in favor of lay citizens while diminishing the power of the state and (in some ways) educational professionals. This line of ideas emphasizes parental empowerment by honoring what Sarason (1994) labels "the political principle" and by recognizing the "historic rights of parents in the education of their children" (Gottfried, 1993, p. 109). It is, at times, buttressed by a strong strand of antiprofessionalism that subordinates "both efficiency and organizational rationality to an emphasis on responsiveness, close public [citizen] control, and local involvement" (Katz, 1971, p. 306).

The ideology of choice is a fourth pillar that will likely support the rebuilt edifice of school governance (Bauman, 1996; Murphy & Shiffman, 2002). Sharing a good deal of space with the concepts of localism, direct democracy, and lay control, choice is designed to "deregulate the demand side of the education market" (Beers & Ellig, 1994, p. 35) and to "enable parents to become more effectively involved in the way the school is run" (Hakim, Seidenstat, & Bowman, 1994, p. 13). It means that "schools would be forced to attend to student needs and parent preferences rather than to the requirements of a centralized bureaucracy" (Hill, 1994, p. 76).

Finally, it seems likely that something that might best be thought of as democratic professionalism will form a central part of the infrastructure of school governance in the postindustrial world. This means the gradual decline of control by elite professionals—by professional managers and more recently by teacher unions—is characterized governance in the industrial era of schooling. Although schools in the industrial era have been heavily controlled by professionals, they have not provided a role for the average teacher in governance. Indeed, under elite democracy and managerial centralization that defined school governance for the past century, teachers were explicitly denied influence. This view of front-line workers is inconsistent with both human capitalism and emerging portraits of postindustrial schooling. It is not surprising, therefore, that the call for an enhanced voice for teachers is a central element in much of the current reform debate. It is also likely to become a key pillar in school governance for tomorrow's schools (Murphy, in press b).

REINVENTING ORGANIZATION AND LEADERSHIP

For some time now, "critics have argued that the reforms of the Progressive Era produced bureaucratic arteriosclerosis—and the low productivity of a declining industry" (Tyack, 1993, p. 3). There is an expanding feeling that the existing structure of administration, which has "changed only a little since the middle of the nineteenth century" (Holmes, 1986, p. 6; National Commission on Teaching and America's Future, 1996) is "obsolete and unsustainable" (Rungeling & Glover, 1991, p. 415). In particular, it is held that the management tools of the bureaucratic paradigm "misdirect the educational outcomes that schools seek to attain" (Wise, 1989, p. 301), that the "bureaucratic structure is failing in a manner so critical that adaptations will not forestall its collapse" (Clark & Meloy, 1989, p. 293). Behind this basic critique rests a central proposition: that "bureaucracies are set up to serve the adults that run them and in the end, the kids get lost in the process" (Daly, cited in Olson, 1992, p. 10). It is increasingly being concluded that the existing bureaucratic system of administration is "ineffective and counterproductive" (Martin & Crossland, 2000, p. 4); that it has "led to teacher isolation, alienation, and disenchantment" (Pellicer & Anderson, 1995, p. 10; Elmore, Peterson, & McCarthy, 1996; Lynch & Strodl, 1991); and that it is "incapable of addressing the technical and structural shortcomings of the public educational system" (Lawton, 1991, p. 4). More finely grained criticism of the bureaucratic infrastructure of schooling comes from a variety of quarters. There are those who contend that schools are so paralyzed by the "bureaucratic arteriosclerosis" noted above by Tyack (1993, p. 3) that "professional judgment" (Hill & Bonan, 1991, p. 65), "innovation" (Lindelow, 1981, p. 98), "morale" (David, 1989, p. 45), "creative capacity" (Snauwaert, 1993, p. 5), flexibility (Elmore et al., 1996), "autonomy" (Shakeshaft, 1999, p. 108), and responsibility and "opportunities for continuing growth" (Howey, 1988, p. 30) have all been paralyzed (Bolin, 1989; Conley, 1989; Frymier, 1987; Sizer, 1984). Other reformers maintain "that school bureaucracies as currently constituted could [never] manage to provide high-quality education" (Elmore, 1993, p. 37) and that, even worse, "bureaucratic management practices have been causing unacceptable distortions in educational process" (Wise, 1989, p. 301), that they are damaging schooling by "interfer[ing] with best teaching" (Johnson, 1989, p. 105) and "getting in the way of children's learning" (Sizer, 1984, p. 206; Cuban, 1989; McNeil, 1988; Wise, 1978). These scholars view bureaucracy as a governance-management system that deflects attention from the core tasks of learning and teaching (Elmore, 1990) and that inhibits the successful conduct of the teaching-learning act (Clark, 1987).

Many analysts also believe that bureaucracy is counterproductive to the needs and interests of educators within the school—"it is impractical, and it does not fit the psychological and personal needs of the workforce" (Clark & Meloy, 1989, p. 293); it "underline[s] the authority of teachers" (Sackney & Dibski, 1992, p. 2); and it is "incompatible with the professional organization" (p. 4). They maintain that "the bureaucratic routinization of teaching and learning that has grown out of administrative attempts to control schools" (Fay, 1992b, p. 58) has neutered teachers (Frymier, 1987), undermined "the drawing power and holding power of strong collegial ties" (Little, 1987, p. 502), and "discourage[d] teachers from taking on additional responsibilities" (Creighton, 1997, p 3). These reviewers contend that "it has become increasingly clear that if we want to improve schools for student learning, we must also improve schools for the adults who work in them" (Smylie & Hart, 1999, p. 421; Clark & Meloy, 1989). Still other critics assert that bureaucratic management is inconsistent with the sacred values and purposes of education; they question "fundamental ideological issues pertaining to bureaucracy's meaning in a democratic society" (Campbell et al., 1987, p. 73) and find that "it is inconsistent to endorse democracy in society but to be skeptical of shared governance in our schools" (Glickman, 1990, p. 74; see also Fusarelli & Scribner, 1993). They maintain that "if the primary purpose of public schools is to support democracy, then schools should be structured around a democratic model" (Katzenmeyer & Moller, 2001, p. 26). As might be expected, given this tremendous attack on the basic organizational infrastructure of schooling, stakeholders at all levels are arguing that "ambitious, if not radical, reforms are required to rectify this situation" (Elmore, 1993, p. 34), and that "the excessively centralized, bureaucratic control of schools must end" (Carnegie Forum, cited in Hanson, 1991, pp. 2–3) and the "outmoded bureaucratic educational structure" (Pellicer & Anderson, 1995, p. 7) must be replaced. There is widespread agreement with the "idea that the 'command and control' approach to educational reform has taken us about as far as it can" (Frost & Durrant, 2003, p. 173). Consequently, a variety of "groups are calling for major changes in the ways schools go about their work" (Lieberman, Saxl, & Miles, 1988, p. 148), changes in the way they are led, and changes in the education of those who lead them (Grogan & Andrews, 2002). New perspectives of schooling include methods of organizing and managing schools that are generally consistent with the "quiet revolution [in] organizational and administrative theory in Western societies" (Foster, 1988, p. 71). In the still-forming image of schools for the 21st century, the hierarchical bureaucratic organizational structures that have defined schooling since the onslaught of scientific management (Forster, 1997) give way to systems that are more focused on capacity building (Crowther, Kaagan, Ferguson, & Hann, 2002) and that are more organic (Weick & McDaniel, 1989), more decentralized (Guthrie, 1986; Harvey & Crandall, 1988; Watkins & Lusi, 1989), and more professionally controlled (David, 1989; Houston, 1989; Weick & McDaniel, 1989), systems that "suggest a new paradigm for school organization and management" (Mulkeen, 1990, p. 105; Fay, 1992a). The basic shift is from a "*power over* approach . . . to a *power to* approach" (Sergiovanni, 1991, p. 57). This model of change spotlights values of community and justice (Murphy, 2002a, 2002b).

In these redesigned, postindustrial school organizations, to which Louis and Miles (1990) have given the label "adaptive model" (p. 26), there are "very basic changes in roles, relationships, and responsibilities" (Seeley, 1988, p. 35): traditional patterns of relationships are altered (Conley, 1989; Rallis, 1990); authority flows are less hierarchical (Clark & Meloy, 1989), for example, traditional distinctions between administrators and teachers begin to blur (Giroux, 1988; Petrie, 1990; Murphy, in press b); role definitions are both more general and more flexible (Corcoran, 1989); and specialization is no longer held in such high regard (Beare, 1989; Houston, 1989) because "organizational structures [will] promote authority based on ability" (Sergiovanni, 1991, p. 62), leadership is dispersed and is connected to competence for needed tasks rather than to formal position (AACTE, 1988; Sykes & Elmore, 1989); and independence and isolation are replaced by cooperative work (Beare, 1989; Maccoby, 1989; Murphy, 1991b). Furthermore, the traditional structural orientation of schools is overshadowed by a focus on the human element (Crow, Hausman, & Scribner, 2002; Louis & Miles, 1990; Sergiovanni, 1991). The operant goal is no longer maintenance of the organizational infrastructure but rather the development of human resources (Clark & Meloy, 1989; Mojkowski & Fleming, 1988; Schlechty, 1990): "Developing teachers [trumps] developing efficient and effective structure" (Silva,

Gimbert, & Nolan, 2000, p. 800). Building learning climates and promoting organizational adaptively replaces the more traditional emphasis on uncovering and applying the one best model of performance (Clark, & Meloy, 1989; McCarthy & Peterson, 1989). A premium is placed on organizational flexibility (Banathy, 1988) and purpose and values (Sergiovanni, 1990, 1992). A new model for school leadership "will create a system driven by the educational needs of students and of society rather than by the imperatives of management accountability systems" (Wise, 1989, p. 310). It will grant that "shared power strengthens the organization" (Livingston, 1992, p. 11). Institutional perspectives no longer dominate the organizational landscape. Rather, schools are reconceptualized as communities (Barth, 2001; Sergiovanni, 1994), "professional workplaces" (Hart, 1995, p. 9), learning organizations (Conley, 1997), and "cooperative systems" (Hart, 1995, p. 10). Notions of schools as "democratic communities" (Katzenmeyer & Moller, 2001, p. 27) and "professional community-oriented images that challenge traditional bureaucratic conceptions of schools as organizations" (Smylie & Hart, 1999, p. 421) move to center stage. Ideas such as "community of leadership" (Barth, 1988, p. 129), the "ethic of collaboration" (Lieberman & Miller, 1999, p. 64), and the principle of care (Beck, 1994) are woven into the fabric of the organization. "The metaphor of the school as community" (Little & McLaughlin, 1993, p. 189) is brightly illuminated (Beck & Foster, 1999; Sergiovanni, 1994). The metaphors being developed for this new design for schools—for example, from principal as manager to principal as facilitator, from teacher as worker to teacher as leader—nicely portray these fundamental revisions in my understanding of social relationships and in my views of organizations and conceptions of management (Beck & Murphy, 1993; Murphy 2002a, 2002b). They reveal a reorientation in transformed schools from bureaucratic to moral authority and from bureaucratic control to professional empowerment, or control through "professional socialization, purposing and shared values, and collegiality and natural interdependence" (Sergiovanni, 1991, p. 60). They also convey an orientation toward accountability through professionalization "rather than through micromanaging what the professional does" (Petrie, 1990, p. 24).

Two themes ribbon the current leadership literature in education. One is "that traditional models of leadership imported from business and industry fall short of the type of leadership required in schools and school districts" (Killion, 1996, p. 64; Sergiovanni, 1990). A second is that "the theoretical orientations that have grounded research on leadership in school organizations" (Pounder, Ogawa, & Adams, 1995, p. 565) leave a good deal to be desired. In short, "the models of school leadership that dominate worldwide are weary, worn, and inadequate" (Crowther et al., 2002, p. xvi). Specifically, academics and practitioners alike increasingly acknowledge that role-based leadership strategies have "dangerously polarized our assumptions about who is responsible for and capable of providing leadership for schools" (Donaldson, 2001, p. 39) and "have been essentially unable to meet the complex challenges associated with school change" (Copland, 2003, pp. 31–32).

Concomitantly, there is a growing belief that "the times are ripe for widening the lens in search of a model of school leadership that is both more productive for schools and more sustainable for those who aspire to lead" (Donaldson, 2001, p. 5), that "rethinking leadership in schools is a crucial first step in moving toward shared, ongoing, and sustainable school improvement" (Copland, 2003, p. 160). There is an acknowledgment that "increasing professionalism, redistributing authority, and increasing collegial interaction redefine school leadership" (Keedy, 1999, p 787). There is a recognition that emerging conceptions of leadership "stress the need to enable, entrust, and empower personnel" (Bishop, Tinley, & Berman, 1997, p. 77) and that "successful organizations depend on multiple sources of leadership" (Childs-Bowen, Moller, & Scrivner, 2000, p. 28; Marks & Printy, 2003). There is an understanding that teachers' "full participation in the work of leadership is necessary for high leadership capacity" (Lambert, 2003, p. 32) and to sustain the leadership of those in formal roles (Donaldson, 2001). In short, "current efforts to redefine leadership are rooted in notions of distribution" (Copland, 2003, p. 161; see especially Elmore, 2000; Sergiovanni, 1984; Spillane, Diamond, & Jita, 2000; Spillane, Halverson, & Diamond, n.d.), in the recognition that "leadership permeates organizations rather than residing in particular people or formal positions of authority" (Smylie, Conley, & Marks, 2000, p. 167; Ogawa & Bossert, 1995; Rallis, 1990). The conception of leadership is one that is non-hierarchical in nature, that is neither predominantly position or authority-based (Ogawa & Bossert, 1995; Sykes & Elmore, 1989)—one in which "leadership is not . . . confused with official position or with exercise of authority" (Foster, 1986, p. 177). Collectively, it bestows less emphasis "upon formal role in the system" (Copland, 2003, p. 160) and less stress on the notion of "legitimate power" (Crowther et al., 2002, p. 23). The new understanding of leadership in play here is "based on expertise" (Keedy, 1999, p. 787) and moral suasion (Fullan, 2004; Greenfield, 1988). Leadership "escapes the role trap" (Pounder, Ogawa, & Adams, 1996, p. 566); it is "authoritative rather than authoritarian" (Forster, 1997, p. 87).

Leadership is defined, at least in part, as an "organizational characteristic" (Hart, 1995, p. 17), "quality" (Ogawa & Bossert, 1995, p. 225), "phenomenon" (Smylie, 1995, p. 6), or "property" (Smylie & Hart, 1999, p. 435). "The capacity to lead is not principal-centric . . . rather embedded in various organizational contexts" (Copland, 2003, p. 162), contexts that formal leaders help create (Firestone, 1996; Rallis, 1990). Leadership is no longer seen as a "zero-sum game" (Pounder, Ogawa, & Adams, 1995, p. 566). Leadership in schools "is not a function of individuals . . . rather it has to do with the mixture of organizational culture and the density of leadership competence among and within many actors" (Copland, 2003, p. 161): "This perspective signals a shift of leadership as the prerogative of an individual to leadership as an organizational property" (Smylie & Hart, 1999, p. 435); "leaders can come from many places and assume many forms" (Crowther et al., 2002, p. 26). Leadership as an organizational property assumes different forms as the viewing prism is turned. In lieu of a focus on roles and positions, some analysts highlight "responsibilit[ies]" (Silva et al., 2000, p. 782), tasks, and "functions that must be performed if the organization is to . . . perform effectively" (Firestone, 1996, p. 396; Spillane et al., n.d.).

Other reviewers spotlight a set of "shared qualities" (Copland, 2003, p. 162). At the heart of all these perspectives is the understanding that "leadership is more collective in nature than individual" (Elmore, 2003, p. 204); "that is, leadership inheres not in the individual characteristics and traits of people in positions of authority, but in the way authority and responsibility are focused, defined, and distributed in organizations" (p. 204). Leadership is cast as a "broad concept, separated from person, role, and a discreet set of individual behaviors" (Copland, 2003, p. 163): "School leadership practice is constituted in the dynamic interaction of multiple leaders . . . and their situation around particular tasks" (Spillane et al., n.d., p. 6). This recast conceptualization of leadership is based on research that "suggest[s] that people in many different roles can lead and thereby affect the performance of their schools" (Pounder, Ogawa, & Adams, 1995, p. 586), "that shared power strengthens the school as an organization" (Stone, Horejs, & Lomas, 1997, p. 50, Heifetz & Laurie, 1997), and that "the accomplishments of a proficient and well-organized group are widely considered to be greater than the accomplishments of isolated individuals" (Little, 1987, p. 495; Retallick & Fink, 2002; Uline & Berkowitz, 2000). Leadership as a shared construct (Chenoweth & Everhart, 2002; Marks & Printy, 2003; Smylie & Hart, 1999) replaces overreliance on hierarchy and bureaucracy (Harrison & Lembeck, 1996; Murphy, in press b) and acknowledges that multiple people "have the opportunity to contribute in meaningful ways" (Wasley, 1991, p. 57). The DNA of shared or distributed leadership—or leadership as an organizational quality—is interactive in design and relational in form (Smylie & Hart, 1999). In the "postheroic era of leadership" (Hart, 1995, p. 10; Fullan, 2004), "collective relationship is replacing the person as the kernel of leadership" (Donaldson, 2001, p. 42) and the "reality of leadership as an interactive rather than a unidirectional process" (Hart, 1995, p. 25) is affirmed: "Leadership is embedded not in particular roles but in the relationships that exist among the incumbents of roles" (Ogawa & Bossert, 1995, p. 235). Leadership "depends more on connections with rather than authority over" (Uline & Berkowitz, 2000, p. 437). The "idea of leadership as relatedness" (Crowther et al., 2002, p. 27) or the tenet that "leadership is a form of relationship among people" (Donaldson, 2001, p. 40), in turn, shifts the focus "away from the individual and toward the interaction patterns among individuals" (Forster, 1997, p. 85). The spotlight is on "interpersonal networks" (Donaldson, 2001, p. 7). The focus is in interactions— "the interact, not the act, becomes the basic building block of organizational leadership" (Ogawa & Bossert, 1995, p. 236).

REINVENTING LEARNING AND TEACHING

From the onset of the industrial revolution, education in the United States has been largely defined by a behavioral psychology-based model of learning—a model that fits nicely with the bureaucratic system of school organization. This viewpoint, in turn, nurtured the development of the

factory and medical practice models of instruction that dominated schooling throughout the 20th century (Schlechty, 1990). Under these two models, the belief that the role of schooling is to sort students into the able and
less able—those who would work with their heads and those who would
work with their hands—has become deeply embedded into the fabric of
schooling (Goodlad, 1984; Powell, Farrar, & Cohen, 1985). According to
Osin and Lesgold (1996), the perspectives noted above have "left the
world with a maladaptive view of learning" (p. 623). What is important
here is the growing belief that we are "in the midst of redefining, even
recreating conceptions of learning and teaching in schools" (Prestine,
1995, p. 140), that is, a shift in the operant model of learning is a fundamental dynamic of the struggle to redefine schools. Of real significance,
if rarely noted, is the fact that this new model reinforces the democratic
tenets embedded in the postindustrial views of governance, organization,
and leadership, discussed above. The behavioral psychology-based model
that highlights the innate capacity of the learner is being challenged by notions of constructivism and situated learning (Cohen, 1988; Prawat & Peterson, 1999; Rowan, 1995) and by the components of authentic pedagogy
(Newmann & Wehlage, 1995). As Prawat and Peterson (1999) inform us,
"Social constructivism represents more than an addition to the traditional,
individualistic perspective that has dominated research on learning for
most of this century. It . . . represents a dramatically different approach to
learning, requiring fundamental changes in how . . . educators think about
the process" (p. 203). Under this approach to learning, schools that historically have been in the business of promoting student adaptation to the
existing social order (Krug, 1964, 1972) are being transformed to ensure
that they "help the vast majority of young people reach levels of skill and
competence once thought within the reach of only a few" (National Commission on Teaching and America's Future, 1996, p. 8). The emerging re-
definition of teaching means that teachers, historically organized to carry
out instructional designs and to implement curricular materials developed
from afar, begin to exercise considerably more control over their profession and the routines of the workplace (Murphy, in press b). Analysts see
this reorganization playing out in a variety of ways at the school level. At
the most fundamental level, teachers have a much more active voice in developing the goals and purposes of schooling—goals that act to delimit or
expand the conception of teaching itself. They also have a good deal more

to say about the curricular structures and pedagogical approaches employed in their schools (Newmann & Wehlage, 1995)—"influence over the basic elements of instructional practice (time, material, student engagement, and so forth)" (Elmore, 1989, p. 20). Finally, teachers demonstrate more control over the supporting ingredients of schooling—such as budgets, personnel, and administration—that affect the way they carry out their responsibilities. Advocates of transformational change also see teaching becoming a more collegial activity (Newmann & Wehlage, 1995). Isolation, so deeply ingrained in the structure and culture of the profession (Lortie, 1975; Rosenholtz, 1989), gives way to more collaborative efforts among teachers (Hargreaves, 1994). At the macro level, teachers are redefining their roles to include collaborative management of the profession, especially providing direction for professional standards. At a more micro level, as noted above, new organizational structures are being created to nurture the development of professional community (Sykes, 1999)—to allow teachers to plan and teach together, to make important decisions about the nature of their roles, and to engage in school-based learning initiatives. As was the case with governance and organization, new views of learning and teaching call for quite different understandings of school leadership and redesigned models of developing school leaders.

6

Consternation within the Profession: Meltdown of the Core

In addition to pressures from the environment, a good deal of internal soul searching has also anchored calls for the reform of school administration and the education of school leaders. As has been the case in other major periods of change in the profession, these concerns have been centered on the two core dimensions of the academy: (a) the intellectual infrastructure supporting the profession, including the research methods used as scaffolding in the construction process, and (b) the methods and procedures used to educate school leaders.

QUESTIONS ABOUT THE INTELLECTUAL INFRASTRUCTURE

In this section, I examine what appears to be an irreparable gash in the fabric of the profession that has acted as a catalyst for the rising turmoil in school administration as well as for the efforts to reshape the profession and the education of its members. I refer specifically to attacks from a variety of quarters on the administration-as-science intellectual foundations that, as I discussed in the first section, grounded the profession from the mid-1950s through the mid-1980s (McCarthy, 1999). Although over the life of the theory movement the profession "increased in formality, structure, and complexity, much as did the school system—from amateur to professional, from simple to complicated, and from intuitive to 'scientific'" (Cooper & Boyd, 1987, p. 7)—the outcomes of the quest for a science of administration were considerably less robust than had been antic-ipated (Donmoyer, 1999; Murphy, 1992). By the mid-1970s, this failure of the theory movement to deliver on its promises was brought to a head in a landmark paper delivered by T. B. Greenfield (1975) at the Third In-ternational Intervisitation Program in Bristol, England (Griffiths, Stout, & Forsyth, 1988b). Although other scholars had been drawing attention to the limitations of a near-exclusive emphasis on a scientific approach to training for some time, Greenfield unleashed the first systemic, broadside attack on the central tenets of the theory movement, especially on its epis-temological roots and guiding values. In a word, he found the scientific era of educational administration to be impoverished. Greenfield's paper went a long way in galvanizing a critique of the field that began to wash over the profession in the mid-1980s. Over the past quarter century, other thoughtful analysts have joined the debate about the appropriate value structure and cognitive base for educational administration (see Culbert-son, 1988; Donmoyer, 1999; Griffiths et al., 1988b; Murphy, 1999d). On the knowledge base issue, there has been increasing agreement—although with noticeable differences in explanations—that "a body of dependable knowledge about educational administration" (Crowson & McPherson, 1987, p. 48) did not emerge during the behavioral science era. This con-dition means that upon exiting the behavioral science era, there was not much "conceptual unity" to the field (Erickson, 1979, p. 9). In practical terms, Erickson concluded that "the field consist[ed] of whatever scholars associated with university programs in 'educational administration' con-sider[ed] relevant. It is, to say the least, amorphous" (p. 9). In his review, Boyan (1988a) concurred, arguing that "the explanatory aspect of the study of administrator behavior in education over 30 years appears to be an incomplete anthology of short stories connected by no particular story line or major themes" (p. 93). Given this absence of conceptual unity, un-til quite recently there has not been much common agreement about the appropriate foundation for the profession (Murphy, 1999d). Thus, as the behavioral science era drew to a close, Goldhammer (1983) reported that although there were "general areas of concern that might dictate to preparatory institutions the names of courses that should be taught . . . there [was] less agreement on what the content of such courses should ac-tually be" (p. 269). At the same time, a pattern of criticism was forming about both the definition of legitimate knowledge and the accepted ways in which it could be generated (Murphy, 1999d). As Crowson and McPherson (1987) reported, during this transition phase, critics "questioned with increasing vigor the appropriateness of traditional research methods and assumptions as a guide to an understanding of practice" (p. 48). Analysts called for both relegitimization of practice-based knowledge and the acceptance of:

> An increasing diversity of research methods, including attempts at qualitative ethnographic, naturalistic, phenomenological, and critical studies . . . [and] an effort to generate "theories of practice" that incorporate both objective and subjective ways of knowing, both fact and value considerations, both "is" and "ought" dimensions of education within integrated frameworks for practice. (Silver, 1982, pp. 56, 53)

Finally, there was a deepening recognition that the knowledge base employed in preparation programs had not been especially useful in solving real problems in the field (Bridges, 1982; Hills, 1975). This questioning of the relevance of theory to practice can be traced to a number of causes. Deeply ingrained methods of working that assumed that one could discover theory that would automatically apply itself to situations of practice was the first. A second was the emergence of a "parochial view of science" (Halpin, 1960, p. 6)—one in which social scientists became "intent upon aping the more prestigious physical scientists in building highly abstract, theoretical models" (p. 6) at the expense of clinical science. A third was the proclivity of educational researchers employing social and behavioral sciences to contribute to the various disciplines rather than to administrative practice—administrative "structure and process were studied mostly as a way of adding to disciplinary domains" (Erickson, 1977, p. 136): "Indeed, the evolution of the field of educational administration reveals a pattern of attempts to resemble and be accepted by the more mature disciplines on campus" (Björk & Ginsberg, 1995, p. 23). Along these same lines, during this entire era was a lack of effort on the part of professors to distinguish systematically those aspects of the social and behavioral sciences that were most appropriate for practitioners (Gregg, 1969). In particular, insufficient attention was directed toward educational organizations as the setting for administration and leadership (Greenfield, 1995). Largely because of the overwhelming nature of the task (Culbertson, 1965), the weakness of the theory movement noted by the American Association of School Administrators (AASA) in 1960—the failure "to work out the essentials in the social sciences for school administrators and to develop a program containing these essentials" (p. 57)—was still a problem as the sun set on the behavioral science era. It remains a problem for the field as we embark on a new millennium in the education of school leaders. A number of critics have also pointed out that regardless of its usefulness, the knowledge base constructed during the scientific era gave rise to a "narrowly defined concept of administration" (Greenfield, 1988, p. 147). This line of analysis spotlights the failure of the profession to include critical concepts, materials, and ideas (Donmoyer, 1999). To begin with, by taking a "neutral posture on moral issues" (Culbertson, 1964, p. 311), the theory movement "actively de-centered morality and values in the quest for a science of organization" (English, 1997, p. 18). When the term *value judgment* did surface, it was "frequently as an epithet indicating intellectual contempt" (Harlow, 1962, p. 66).

Throughout the behavioral science era, there was "little serious, conscious effort to develop demonstrably in students the skills or behavioral propensities to act in ways that could be considered ethical" (Farquhar, 1981, p. 199; Beck & Murphy, 1994). Attention to the "humanities as a body of 'aesthetic wisdom' capable of contributing its own unique enrichment to the preparation of school administrators" (Popper, 1982, p. 12) was conspicuous by its absence. Also neglected during this period of administration qua administration were educational issues (Murphy, 1992)—a phenomenon exacerbated by efforts to professionalize administration and thereby distinguish it from teaching (Murphy, Hallinger, Lotto, & Miller, 1987). What Anderson and Lonsdale reported in 1957—that "few items in the literature of educational administration . . . say much about the psychology of learning" (p. 429)—and what Boyan concluded in 1963—that "the content of the advanced preparation tends to focus on the managerial and institutional dimensions as compared to teaching, the technical base of educational organizations" (pp. 3–4)—were still true in the mid-1990s as the dialectic era of school administration began to lay down roots (Murphy, 1990c, 1999d).

In summary, by the early 1990s, a multifaceted assessment of the intellectual foundations of the profession had produced a good deal of disquiet in the profession (Donmoyer, Imber, & Scheurich, 1995). This unease, in turn, has continually fueled the turmoil that still characterizes the academic wing of the field. It has also served—directly and indirectly—as a springboard for many of the reform initiatives that have sprung up in the profession, especially around the preparation and professional development functions.

CONCERNS ABOUT PREPARATION PROGRAMS

The current era of rebuilding is fueled not only by critique of the intellectual foundations of the profession but also by critical reviews of preparation programs for school leaders (see, for example, Griffiths, Stout, & Forsyth, 1988; Murphy, 1990b, 1992). Reviewers have chronicled a system of preparing school leaders that is seriously flawed and that has been found wanting in nearly every aspect. Specifically, critics have uncovered serious problems in (a) the ways students are recruited and selected into training programs; (b) the education they receive once there—including the content emphasized and the pedagogical strategies employed; (c) the methods used to assess academic fitness; and (d) the procedures developed to certify and select principals and superintendents. My review focuses on concerns that helped fuel the emergence of the ferment of the 1980s and 1990s.

Recruitment and Selection

Analyses conducted throughout the most recent period of ferment of the recruitment and selection processes employed by institutions in the administrator training business consistently found them lacking in rigor. Procedures were often informal, haphazard, and casual. Prospective candidates were often self-selected, and there were few leader recruitment programs. Fewer than 10% of students reported that they were influenced by the recruitment activities of the training institutions. Despite well-documented, if commonsensical, reminders that training outcomes depended on the mix of program experiences and the quality of entering students (Creighton, 2002), research on the recruitment of school administrators was quite anemic (American Association of Colleges for Teacher Education, 1988; Miklos, 1988). Standards for selecting students into preparation programs were often perfunctory: "Most programs ha[d] 'open admissions,' with a baccalaureate degree the only prerequisite"

(Griffiths et al., 1988b, p. 290); "For too many administrator preparation programs, any body is better than no body" (Jacobson, 1990, p. 35).

The University Council for Educational Administration (UCEA)-sponsored study of the mid-1970s (Silver, 1978a) discovered that the rejection rates to preparation programs were quite low—about 12% for master's students, 14% for sixth-year students, and 25% for doctoral students. In 1984, Gerritz, Koppich, & Guthrie found that only about 1 in 30 applicants was denied admission to certification programs in California. Part of the reason for this nonselectivity can be traced to the use of questionable methods and procedures and to poorly articulated standards for entry. If all one needed 50 years ago to enter a training program in educational administration was a "B.A. and the cash to pay tuition" (Tyack & Cummings, 1977, p. 60), the situation was not much improved as the profession took stock of itself throughout the 1980s and 1990s. It is not surprising that the quality of applicants is, and has been for some time, rather low. In 1988, for instance, Griffiths et al. (1988b) revealed that "of the 94 intended majors listed in [the] Guide to the Use of the Graduate Record Examination Program 1985–86 . . . educational administration is fourth from the bottom" (p. 12). This lack of rigorous recruitment and selection procedures and criteria has several negative effects.

> First, it lowers the level of training and experience possible, since courses are often geared to the background and intelligence of the students. Second, "eased entry downgrades the status of the students in the eyes of the populace." Third, the candidates themselves realize that anyone can get in and that nearly everyone will get the license if he or she just keeps paying for credits. In part, this lack of rigor at entry reflects a lack of clear criteria for training or clear vision of what candidates and graduates will look like, and the realization that the graduate school experience itself is not very demanding. (Cooper & Boyd, 1987, p. 14)

This lack of rigor was believed to be contributing to the serious oversupply of credentialed administrators in the United States.

Program Content

Turning to the content of preparation programs at the time the ferment in the profession was richly bubbling, critical reviews revealed the following problems: the indiscriminate adoption of practices untested and uninformed by educational values and purposes; serious fragmentation; the separation of the practice and academic arms of the profession; relatively nonrobust strategies for generating new knowledge; the neglect of ethics; an infatuation with the study of administration for its own sake; and the concomitant failure to address outcomes.

Critics averred that in many preparation programs "course content [was] frequently banal" (Clark, 1988, p. 5). Nor did training programs exhibit much internal consistency. Students often confronted a "confusing melange of courses, without clear meaning, focus, or purpose" (Cooper & Boyd, 1987, p. 14; see also Achilles, 1984). There was an absence of a "continuum of knowledge and skills that become more sophisticated as one progress[ed]" (Peterson & Finn, 1985, pp. 51–52). What all this meant was "that most administrators receiv[ed] fragmented, overlapping, and often useless courses that add[ed] up to very little" (Cooper & Boyd, 1987, p. 13). One of the most serious problems with the cognitive base in school administration training programs was that it did not reflect the realities of the workplace (Lakomski, 1998; Murphy, 1990b) and was therefore, at best, "irrelevant to the jobs trainees assume[d]" (Mulkeen & Cooper, 1989, p. 1) and, at worst, "dysfunctional in the actual world of practice" (Sergiovanni, 1989, p. 18). As I reported earlier, scholars of the behavioral science era attempted to develop a science of administration. One of the effects was an exacerbation of the natural tension between the practice and academic arms of the profession. The nurturance and development of the social sciences became ends in themselves. Professors, never very gifted at converting scientific knowledge to the guidance of practice, had little motivation to improve. As a result, the theory and research borrowed from the behavioral sciences "never evolved into a unique knowledge base informing the practice of school administration" (Griffiths et al., 1988a, p. 19). Mann (1975), Bridges (1977), Muth (1989), Sergiovanni (1989), and others have all written influential essays in which they describe how the processes and procedures stressed in university programs as we transitioned into the dialectic era were often diametrically opposed to conditions that characterize the workplace milieu of schools. Other thoughtful reviewers concluded that administrators-in-training were often "given a potpourri of theory, concepts, and ideas—unrelated to one another and rarely useful in either understanding schools or managing them" (Mulkeen & Cooper, 1989, p. 12). For example, in their review of training programs at the end of the theory era, Crowson and McPherson (1987) argued that institutions "that had emphasized a solid grounding in theory, the social sciences, [and] rational decision making . . . were discovered to be well off the mark as effective preparation for the chaotic life of a principal or superintendent" (p. 49).

Evidence from nearly all fronts led to the conclusion that the focus on the behavioral sciences during the scientific era of training resulted in a glaring absence of consideration of the problems faced by practicing school administrators (Murphy, 1999b; McCarthy, 1999). The pervasive antirecipe, antiskill philosophy that characterized many programs of educational administration resulted in significant gaps in the prevailing knowledge base: an almost complete absence of performance-based program components, a lack of attention to practical problem-solving skills, "a neglect of practical intelligence" (Sergiovanni, 1989, p. 17), and a truncated conception of expertise. Administrators consistently reported that the best way to improve training in preparation programs would be to improve the instruction on job-related skills (Erlandson & Witters-Churchill, 1988). The clinical aspects of most preparation programs in educational administration heading into the 21st century were notoriously weak. Despite an entrenched belief that supervised practice "could be the most critical phase of the administrator's preparation" (Griffiths et al., 1988a, p. 17) and a long history of efforts to make field-based learning an integral part of preparation programs, little progress had been made in this area. And despite concern over the impoverished nature of clinical experience for nearly 30 years, Pepper was still able to report in 1988 that "few, if any, university programs in school administration offer a thorough clinical experience for future school administrators" (p. 361).

The field-based component continued to be infected with weaknesses that have been revisited on a regular basis since the first decade of the behavioral science revolution in administrative preparation: (a) unclear objectives; (b) inadequate number of clinical experiences; (c) activities arranged on the basis of convenience; (d) overemphasis on role-centered as opposed to problem-centered experiences; (e) lack of individualization; (f) poor planning, supervision, and follow-up; (g) absence of "connecting linkages between on-campus experiences and field-based experiences" (Milstein, 1990, p. 121); and (h) overemphasis on low-level (orientation and passive observation type) activities (McKerrow, 1998; Milstein, 1996). Woven deeply into the fabric of "administration as an applied science" was the belief that there was a single best approach to educating prospective school leaders (Cooper & Boyd, 1987), including a dominant world view of administration as an area of study (content) and method of acting (procedure). A number of thoughtful analysts maintain that this perspective has resulted in significant gaps in the knowledge base employed in training programs. Missing was consideration of the diversity of perspectives that informed scholarship and practice. For example, in her review of the literature on women administrators, Shakeshaft (1988) discovered "differences between the ways men and women approach the tasks of administration" (p. 403). She concluded that, although "these differences have implications for administrative training programs . . . the female world of administrators has not been incorporated into the body of work in the field . . . [n]or are women's experiences carried into the literature on practice" (p. 403–406; see also 1999). Similar conclusions were reached about racial minorities.

As noted, one of the most troubling aspects of preparation programs exiting the behavioral science era was that they had very little to do with education (Murphy, 1990b, 1990c). Most programs showed "little interest in exploring the historical roots and social context of schooling" (Anderson, 1990, p. 53) and did "a very bad job of teaching . . . a wider vision of schools in society" (Mulkeen & Cooper, 1989, p. 12). Furthermore, there was ample evidence that the content in training programs was heavily influenced by the "pervasive managerial-administrative ethic" (Evans, 1998, p. 30) that undergirded the profession and that preparation programs largely ignored matters of teaching and learning, of pedagogy and curriculum (Murphy, 1992). Most of the interest and scholarly activity of the behavioral science era heavily reinforced the "separation of problems in administration from problems in education" (Greenfield, 1988, p. 144) and the emphasis on noneducational issues in training programs. As Evans (1991) astutely chronicled, the focus was on discourse and training primarily on "the administration of education" (p. 3), or administration qua administration—a major shift from its formative years when the emphasis "was upon the adjective 'educational' rather than upon the noun 'administration'" (Guba, 1960, p. 115). The separation of educational administration "from the phenomenon known as instruction" (Er-

ickson, 1979, p. 10) meant that the typical graduate of a school administration training program could act only as "a mere spectator in relation to
the instructional program" (Hills, 1975, p. 4).

By the early 1960s, the second major root of the field—values and
ethics—like education before it, had atrophied (Beck & Murphy, 1994).
The result was reduced consideration of two issues: (a) organizational values, purpose, and ethics and (b) organizational outcomes. According to
Greenfield (1988), "The empirical study of administrators has eluded their
moral dimensions and virtually all that lends significance to what they do"
(p. 138). Despite some early notices that "educational administration requires a distinctive value framework" (Graff & Street, 1957, p. 120), despite pleas to reorient administration toward purposing (Harlow, 1962),
and despite clear reminders that education is fundamentally a moral activity (Culbertson, 1963; Halpin, 1960), the issue of meaning in school administration as a profession and in its training programs had taken a back
seat "to focus upon the personality traits of administrators—upon the
mere characteristics of administrators rather than upon their character"
(Greenfield, 1988, pp. 137–138). Thus, at the close of the theory era, administrators were exiting training programs unprepared to grapple with
ethical issues (Rusch, 2003) or to address openly the values deeply embedded in schools that often hide behind "a mask of objectivity and im-
partiality" (Thurpp, 2003, p. 150). As early as 1960, Chase was pointing
out what was to become an increasingly problematic situation in educational administration in general and in training programs in particular—a
lack of concern for outcomes. Seventeen years later, Erickson (1977) reported that studies in the field "between 1954 and 1974 provided no
adequate basis for outcome-oriented organizational strategy in education"
(p. 128). Two years later, Erickson (1979) expanded on the ideas of his
earlier essay. He documented "the tendency to neglect the careful tracing
of connections between organizational variables and student outcomes"
(p. 12). He decried the focus on the characteristics of administrators at the
expense of more useful work. He laid out his now famous line of attack
on the problem: "The current major emphasis in studies of organizational
consequences should be on postulated causal networks in which student
outcomes are the bottom line" (p. 12). As the 21st century approached,
preparation programs had yet to resonate to this idea. Indeed, in their
analysis using data available at the start of the current era of ferment (i.e.,

1986–1987), Haller, Brent, and McNamara (1997) concluded that "taken collectively, graduate programs in educational administration seem to have little or no influence on the attributes that characterize effective schools" (p. 227; see also Brent, 1998).

Delivery System

The delivery system that shaped preparation programs at the tail end of the theory movement and inception of the dialectic era was marked by a number of serious problems, most of which have a long history. Looking at the profession as a whole, it is clear that too many institutions are involved in the training business. At the time of the National Commission on Excellence in Educational Administration (1987) report, there were 505 institutions offering course work in educational leadership, with "less than 200 hav[ing] the resources and commitment to provide the excellence called for by the Commission" (p. 20). Many of these programs were cash cows for their sponsoring universities, kept open more for political and economic than for educational reasons. In 1983, Willower offered this assessment of the situation: Many "offer graduate study in name only. They seriously stint inquiry and survive by offering easy credentials and by working hard at legislative politics. Their faculties neither contribute to the ideas of the field nor are they actively engaged with them" (p. 194). These institutions tended to be characterized by high student–faculty ratios and limited specialization among faculty.

A related problem was the framework in which students' educational experiences unfolded: "Administrator training . . . [was] most often a dilatory option, pursued on a convenience basis, part-time, on the margins of a workday" (Sykes & Elmore, 1989, p. 80). Programs had indeed drifted far from the traditional residency model. At the end of the 1970s, Silver (1978a) reported that "the ideal of one or two years of full-time student life at the graduate level seems to be disappearing from our preparatory programs, and with it the notions of time for scholarly objectivity, student life, and colleague-like interaction between professors and students" (pp. 207–208). As many as 95 percent of all students were part-timers (Griffiths et al., 1988b), and "many students complet[ed] their training . . . without forming a professional relationship with a professor or student colleague" (Clark, 1988, p. 5).

The profession entered the third era of ferment with the arts and science model of education firmly entrenched in schools of education and departments of school administration—to, the critics held, the detriment of the profession (Griffiths et al., 1988a). According to them, this arts and science framework emerged more to help professors develop "greater academic sophistication through their professional roles in order to gain acceptance by their peers in other departments" (Goldhammer, 1983, p. 256) than to respond to the needs of prospective administrators. Unfortunately, it was clear by the 1990s that the model had neither furnished professors the status for which they had hoped nor provided graduates with the tools they needed in order to be successful practitioners (Björk & Ginsberg, 1995). In addition, it had driven a wedge between professors and practitioners, creating what Goldhammer (1983) labeled the "university-field gap" (p. 265).

The emulation of the arts and science model had spawned a number of subproblems in preparation programs. One of the most serious was that education designed for practitioners (Ed.D. programs) had been molded to parallel the training provided to researchers (Ph.D. programs), in terms of both research requirements (Silver, 1978b) and general course work (Norton & Levan, 1987). This blurring of requirements and experiences for students pursuing quite distinct careers resulted in the development of ersatz research programs for prospective practitioners. Students, burdened with a variety of inappropriate activities, were being prepared to be neither first-rate researchers nor successful practitioners. In attempting to address the need to develop intradepartmental balance between professor-scholars attuned to the disciplines and professor-practitioners oriented to the field, departments had by the start of the dialectic era generally produced the worst of both. Unclear about the proper mission of preparation programs, seeking to enhance the relatively low status afforded professors of school administration, and overburdened with multitudes of students, faculties in educational leadership were characterized by an anti-intellectual bias (Griffiths, 1997), weak scholarship (McCarthy et al., 1988), problematic connections to the field (Willower, 1988), and considerable resistance to change (Cooper & Muth, 1994; McCarthy et al., 1988; Murphy, 1991a). A number of reviewers concluded that "only a relatively small number of those in the field of educational administration [were] actively engag[ed] in scholarly activities" (Immegart, 1990, p. 11). Even more disheartening were the assessments of the quality of the scholarship at the time (Boyan, 1981). According to Hawley (1988), because of serious limitations in their own training, many professors were not qualified to supervise research. Coupling this deficiency in ability with the previously noted lack of effort resulted in a situation in which "very little good research was being conducted by [educational administration] faculty and students" (Hawley, 1988, p. 85) and in which students developed a truncated, academic view of scholarly inquiry.

It is probably not surprising, although it is distressing, that, as we moved into the 21st century, inappropriate content ineffectively packaged was also being poorly delivered in many training institutions. "The dominant mode of instruction continu[ed] to be lecture and discussion in a classroom setting based on the use of a textbook" (Mulkeen & Tetenbaum, 1990, p. 20). Although some progress was made during the behavioral science era to infuse reality-oriented instructional strategies into preparation programs, the change was hardly revolutionary, and the use of innovative pedagogical methods was not prevalent at the close of the theory movement in school administration. For example, in the Texas National Association of Secondary School Principals (NASSP) study (Erlandson & Witters-Churchill, 1988), principals reported "lecture and discussion" to be the primary instructional mode used for eight of nine skill areas examined—and for the ninth skill, written communication, it was a close second!

Standards

Thoughtful critique of preparation programs into the late 1990s revealed that the lack of rigorous standards was a serious problem that touched almost every aspect of educational administration. Previously, I noted the general absence of standards at the point of entry into preparation programs. According to critics, once students entered preparation programs, the situation did not improve: "The quality of [their] experiences [was] often abysmally low" (Mulkeen & Cooper, 1989, p. 1). They were not exposed to rigorous coursework: "Students mov[ed] through the program without ever seeing a current research study (other than a local dissertation), without ever having read an article in *ASQ* or *EAQ* or *AJS* (*Administrative Science Quarterly, Educational Administration Quarterly*, and

American Journal of Sociology, respectively). They [were] functionally il-
literate in the basic knowledge of our field" (Clark, 1988, pp. 4–5). Because performance criteria were ill-defined, there was also very little
monitoring of student progress (Hawley, 1988). Not surprisingly, very few
entrants into certification programs failed to complete their programs for
academic reasons. Most former students indicated that their graduate
training was not very rigorous (Jacobson, 1990; Muth, 1989). The delivery system most commonly employed—part-time study in the evening or
on weekends—resulted in students who came to their "studies worn-out,
distracted, and harried" (Mann, 1975, p. 143) and contributed to the
evolution and acceptance of low standards (Hawley, 1988). Exit requirements, in turn, were often "slack and unrelated to the work of the
profession" (Peterson & Finn, 1985, p. 54). Compounding the lack of
standards at almost every phase of preparation programs were university
faculty who were unable or unwilling to improve the situation (Hawley,
1988; McCarthy et al., 1988). Even greater obstacles to improving standards were the bargains, compromises, and treaties that operated in preparation programs—the lowering of standards in exchange for high enroll-
ments and compliant student behavior. Thus, not surprisingly, reviewers
argued that the time had come to markedly elevate standards in school
administration.

Program Evaluation

In 1946, Grace identified an important gap in the preparation architecture
—a lack of work devoted to the examination of the effectiveness of educational programs in school administration. He held that institutions of
higher education needed to be more diligent in assessing program quality
and impact. The call for greater attention to program assessment was
picked up in the 1950s by Wynn (1957), in the 1960s by Gregg (1960,
1969), and in the 1970s by Farquhar (1977) and Silver (1978a, 1978b).
Over the past quarter century, other scholars have periodically spotlighted
the need for action on this line of work. Yet this particular patch of the research landscape in the school administration has lain fallow. At the dawn
of the 21st century, Glasman, Cibulka, and Ashby (2002) summed up the
situation somewhat charitably for the National Commission on the Advancement of Educational Leadership Preparation as follows: "Educational

leadership programs have not had a strong tradition of engagement in self evaluation of their programs" (p. 258).

TRENDS IN THE REFORM OF PREPARATION PROGRAMS: MARKERS ON THE PATH TO REFORM

In this section, I review the key markers on this road to more productive preparation programs, and I tease out reform trends. Although it is impossible to prejudge what future historians of educational administration will designate as the specific major events that helped shape the education of school leaders for the post-theory era, certain events appear likely to receive considerable attention. An overview of significant events follows.

One marker that will surely be singled out is the set of activities comprising the work of the National Commission on Excellence in Educational Administration (NCEEA). Growing out of the deliberations of the Executive Council of the University Council for Educational Administration, the commission was formed in 1985 under the direction of Daniel E. Griffiths. The NCEEA produced three influential documents that promoted considerable discussion both within and outside educational administration: the 1987 report *Leaders for America's Schools*; Griffiths' highly influential address to the 1988 annual meeting of the American Educational Research Association (AERA) (subsequently published as a UCEA paper [Griffiths et al., 1988a]), and a UCEA-sponsored edited volume containing most of the background papers commissioned by the NCEEA (Griffiths et al., 1988a). These three documents helped to crystallize the sense of what was wrong with the profession in general and with the preparatory function specifically, to extend discussion about possible solutions, and, to a lesser extent, to provide signposts for those engaged in redefining school administration and rebuilding preparation programs.

Following up on these activities, then UCEA executive director, Patrick Forsyth, set about mustering support for one of the key NCEEA recommendations—the creation of the National Policy Board for Educational Administration (NPBEA). After considerable work on the part of UCEA, the NPBEA was created in 1988. The NPBEA has undertaken a series of activities designed to provide direction for the reconstruction of the profession, especially its training function. NPBEA released its first report, titled *Improving the Preparation of School Administrators: The Reform Agenda*, in May 1989. The report outlines an extensive overhaul and strengthening of preparation programs. Its recommendations were later adopted in slightly modified form by the universities comprising the UCEA. Following the release of *The Reform Agenda*, the NPBEA published a series of occasional papers that were designed to inform the reform debate on preparing the next generation of school leaders. It also sponsored, in conjunction with the Danforth Foundation, national conferences to help professors discover alternatives to deeply ingrained practices in training programs. Its 1992 conference on problem-based learning drew nearly 150 participants from universities throughout the United States and Canada.

Building on earlier-noted documents, two national efforts to redefine the knowledge base undergirding preparation unfolded in the early 1990s. In 1990, the National Commission for the Principalship (NCP), under the leadership of Scott D. Thomson, published a report titled *Principals for Our Changing Schools: Preparation and Certification*. The document represents an attempt to unpack the functional knowledge base required by principals. Working from this document, Thomson, under the aegis of the NPBEA—of which he was, at the time, executive secretary—assigned teams to flesh out each of the 21 knowledge domains identified in the report. The resulting document, *Principals for Our Changing Schools: The Knowledge and Skill Base* (NCP, 1993) provides a comprehensive outline of the core knowledge and skills needed by principals to lead today's schools. A year later, the UCEA authorized six writing teams under the overall direction of Wayne K. Hoy to update the knowledge bases in educational administration preparation programs.

In addition to the reform reports described earlier, change efforts have been shaped by a series of volumes devoted to the analysis and improvement of the academic arm of the profession and its preparation programs. Each of these books has helped focus attention on the problems of the field and has provided alternative visions for a post-theory world as well as solution paths to guide the voyage. Some of the most important of these volumes are the first two handbooks of research in the field, AERA-sponsored volumes, edited by Boyan (1988b) and Murphy & Louis (1999)—the *Handbook of Research on Educational Administration*; two volumes on the professoriate, authored by Martha M. McCarthy and colleagues—a 1988 book titled *Under Scrutiny: The Educational Administration Professoriate* and a 1997 follow-up volume, with G. D. Kuh—*Continuity and Change: The Educational Leadership Professoriate*; the edited volume growing out of the NCEEA project—*Leaders for America's Schools* (Griffiths et al., 1988a); two National Society for the Study of Education yearbooks—*Educational Leadership and Changing Contexts of Families, Communities, and Schools* (Mitchell & Cunningham, 1990), and *The Educational Leadership Challenge: Redefining Leadership for the 21st Century* (Murphy, 2002a); a volume resulting from the National Center for Educational leadership conference on cognitive perspectives in school administration—*Cognitive Perspectives on Educational Leadership* (Hallinger, Leithwood, & Murphy, 1993); and a volume on school administration published by the Politics of Education Association and edited by Hannaway and Crowson (1989)—*The Politics of Reforming School Administration*.

Other books devoted primarily to the reform of preparation programs include those edited by Murphy in 1993—*Preparing Tomorrow's School Leaders: Alternative Designs*; Mulkeen, Cambron-McCabe, and Anderson in 1994—*Democratic Leadership: The Changing Context of Administrative Preparation*; Donmoyer, Imber, and Scheurich in 1995—*The Knowledge Base in Educational Administration: Multiple Perspectives*; and Murphy and Forsyth in 1999—*Educational Administration: A Decade of Reform*; and those authored by Beck in 1994—*Reclaiming Educational Administration as a Caring Profession*; Beck and Murphy in 1994—*Ethics in Educational Leadership Preparation Programs: An Expanding Role*—and in 1997 (Beck, Murphy, & Associates, 1997a)—*Ethics in Educational Leadership Programs: Emerging Models*; Milstein and Associates in 1993—*Changing the Way We Prepare Educational Leaders: The Danforth Experience*; and Murphy in 1992—*The Landscape of Leadership Preparation: Reframing the Education of School Administrators*.

A particularly influential marker coming at the back end of the third era of turmoil was Murphy's 1999 invited AERA address (later published as a UCEA monograph) on the state of the profession of school administration—*The Quest for a Center: Notes on the State of the Profession of Educational Leadership* (1999d). Based on a comprehensive review of work underway throughout the field, the *Quest* document directs the profession to rebuild itself not on updated revisions of traditional blueprints but rather on the valued ends of schooling—school improvement, social justice, and democratic community.

As noted, the initiatives of the Danforth Foundation in the 1980s and 1990s will no doubt been seen as an important marker in this period of reform. In addition to its sponsorship of the NCEEA and its core support for the NPBEA, Danforth underwrote four significant efforts designed to assist self-analyses and preparation program improvement efforts in educational administration, all of which capture multiple elements from the various reform volumes and documents of the late 1980s: (a) a Principals' Program to improve preparation programs for prospective leaders; (b) a Professors' Program to enhance the capability of departments to respond to needed reforms; (c) research and development efforts, such as the Problem-Based Learning Project, which designed alternative approaches to understanding the profession and to educating tomorrow's leaders; and (d) a series of conferences and workshops created to help the professoriate grapple with important reform ideas in the area of preparing leaders for tomorrow's schools.

Standards-defining activities are also likely to be heavily referenced in future reports of events shaping the evolution, and perhaps the transformation, of preparation programs in school leadership. The central line of activity here revolves around the work of the Interstate School Leaders Licensure Consortium (ISLLC). Created in the mid-1990s by the NPBEA and chaired by Joseph Murphy of Vanderbilt University, this group of 24 states and major professional associations developed the first universal set of standards for school leaders. Approved late in 1996, the ISLLC Standards for School Leaders have been adopted or adapted for use in 40 states as the basis for operating preparation programs. In addition, 14 states currently use the ETS-developed, standards-based "School Leaders Licensure Assessment" to license graduates of preparation programs. Equally important, on the professional front, the ISLCC Standards have been adopted by NCATE as their standards for accrediting preparation programs, thus significantly enhancing their influence on the preparation of school leaders (Murphy, in press a; Murphy & Shipman, 1999; Murphy, Yff, & Shipman, 2000).

Histories of the field of school administration reveal two conclusions about foundational support (Campbell et al., 1987; Murphy, 1992). On the one hand, there has not been much of it. On the other hand, the resources that have been forthcoming have exerted an important influence on the academic arm of school leadership in general and on preparation programs in particular.[*] This was true in the 1950s when the Kellogg Foundation supported the highly influential Cooperative Project in Educational Administration. It held again in the 1980s and 1990s when Danforth Foundation support helped nudge preparation programs from a foundation of complacency and reset them on much stronger pillars (McCarthy, 1999; Milstein & Associates, 1993). My reading of the existing clues leads me to conclude that the current "third wave" of foundational support will also be identified in future reports as a key marker in the existing reform environment. Here, in particular, I note three initiatives of the Wallace Foundation: (a) the funding of a series of comprehensive studies to gain a fuller understanding of the types of leadership that promote student success, (b) an investigation into the elements of high-quality preparation programs, and (c) the creation of the State Action for Education Leadership Project (SAELP) through which some states (e.g., Missouri and Montana) are employing state policy in the service of strengthening preparation programs, either by creating new training avenues or by upgrading existing pathways. In a similar vein, the Broad Foundation is supporting the creation of alternative models of preparation such as New Leaders for New Schools. A central dynamic of this new round of philanthropy is that unlike earlier funding that employed professionally based reform strategies, market or political change engines are featured here. The founding of the *Journal of School Leadership* (*JSL*) in 1991 will likely be noted as a significant thread in the preparation reform fabric. This is the case because *JSL* publishes a significantly higher percentage of articles on preparation programs than do the other journals on school administration—*Educational Administration Quarterly* (*EAQ*), *Journal of Educational Administration* (*JEA*), and *Planning and Changing* (Murphy & Vriesenga, 2004). Finally, it is likely that recent actions by AERA and UCEA will stand the test of time when the history of administrator preparation is written. For AERA, the important events were the establishment of the special interest groups on teaching and learning in educational administration and on problem-based learning. For UCEA, one major marker was the development of an annual convention in 1987 with significant attention devoted to issues of preparation. The other major initiative was the creation under the leadership of Executive Director Michelle Young of the National Commission on the Advancement of Educational Leadership Preparation (NCAELP) in 2001. Working in cooperation with the NPBEA, NCAELP is engaged in a comprehensive project to (a) develop a complex understanding of contemporary contextual factors impacting educational leadership and leadership preparation, (b) examine exceptional and innovative educational leadership preparation and professional development programs, (c) determine clearly and precisely what must take place both within and outside the university to ensure effective educational leadership preparation and professional development, and (d) create a comprehensive and collaborative set of action plans for the future. Commission members working under the guidance of Professor Young are engaged in a series of preparation program reform efforts (see special issue of *Educational Administration Quarterly*, 2002, *38*[2], especially Young and Peterson, 2002, as well as Grogan and Andrews, 2002).

My understanding of actual changes underway in preparation programs in school leadership is constructed from information from four areas of work. Chronicles of reformation in individual programs or groups of departments engaged in related reforms provide the richest repository of knowledge to date. Second, but less prevalent, are analyses of activities on specific pieces of the reform agenda (e.g., cohort programs, problem-based instructional strategies, the use of technology). Treatments of the strategies that important professional bodies have used to reshape the profession furnish a third useful lens for drawing conclusions about changes afoot in departments of educational leadership. Finally, there are a number of macrolevel analyses of the recontoured landscape of the profession. These, in turn, are of two types: synthetic reviews and empirical studies. Building on this collective work, I discern that some distinct patterns in the reform of preparation programs have begun to emerge in the last few years (see Murphy, 1993, 1999a, 1999b, 1999d, 2002a, 2002b; Murphy & Forsyth, 1999; Murphy & Vriesenga, 2004). I review the most important of these trends below, concentrating on those with deepest roots and/or with greatest implications for the redevelopment of the preparation function.

I begin, however, with a few cautionary notes to guide these analyses. In *Life on the Mississippi*, Mark Twain reminds us that "[p]artialities often make people see more than really exists." Thus, an analysis of trends in preparation could encourage the reader to arrive at firmer conclusions than might be desirable. A thoughtful review of the history of innovation in preparation programs for school leaders would lead one to be careful here. The literature is replete with inaccurate claims of the importance and the magnitude of incipient movements in the training of school adminis-trators. Whether or not the changes described herein represent the crest of a wave that will break across all of educational leadership is an empirical question that can be answered only at some time in the future. Even if my inchoate chronicle here faithfully portrays the right set of actors and themes, it is difficult to imagine that the storyline will not evolve over time, changing in ways that will, perhaps, make them unrecognizable to today's viewers.

At the risk of insulting the reader, I also take a moment to state the ob-vious. That is, the full portfolio of trends as well as the individual patterns I unpack below can be traced to the "Change Forces" described in earlier chapters and the platform of ideas surfaced in the documents outlined in the previous section on "Markers on the Path to Reform."

An Awakening: New Energy for Reform Work

One central conclusion of my analysis is that considerable energy is flow-ing into the reformation of preparation programs in school administration. A second finding is that the pressure is having a noticeable impact on the preparatory structure in the area of school leadership and on administra-tor preparation programs.

Earlier reports on the readiness of the field for change in its preparation programs were disheartening. Studies by McCarthy and her colleagues (McCarthy et al., 1988; McCarthy & Kuh, 1997) and by Murphy (1991a) found a general level of complacency about preparation programs among professors of educational administration. The assumption of the profes-sion of a more active stance (see Murphy, 1999b, 1999a) is, therefore, worthy of note. I expect that time is one variable in play in this shift in ex-pectations. That is, unlike in the earlier studies, most of the reform reports in the area of leadership have had a chance to spread across the profes-sion. There has also been sufficient time for programs to engage change initiatives and for some of those efforts to take root.

It may also be the case that the buffering these programs have histori-cally enjoyed — buffering employed to fend off external influences — may be thinning considerably. In short, their option not to act may be becoming reduced. In particular, the resurgence of more vigorous state control over preparation programs may be propelling reform efforts. This has certainly been the case in states, such as North Carolina, Mississippi, Kentucky, Delaware, and New Jersey. Concomitantly, the introduction of market dynamics into the licensure system may be influencing departments to strengthen training programs (Murphy & Hawley, 2003). At least two such forces have surfaced over the past decade—the creation of alternative avenues for licensure and the growth of alternative providers of programs leading to licensure, especially those offered by professional associations, local educational agencies, and entrepreneurial developers.

Professional forces may also lie behind recent reform work. There is a sense that the earlier widespread complacency about preparation programs among professors of educational administration is being challenged as older members of the professoriate retire and new faculty begin to assume the reins of the profession. If, indeed, we are witnessing a lifting of the veil of complacency, it may be attributable to the influx of more women professors and of more faculty members who are joining the professoriate from practice (McCarthy, 1999) than was the case in earlier decades.

The growth of professional groups dedicated to program reform, such as the new AERA special interest groups on problem-based learning, as well as teaching and learning in educational administration, are noteworthy markers in the professional area. So, too, has been the development of professional networks of reformers, such as those nurtured through the Danforth initiatives of the late 1980s and early 1990s and the work of Kottkamp and Orr on program evaluation and Marshall on social justice over the last few years. In short, it may be that the rather inhospitable landscape of the profession is being remolded to be more receptive to the seeds of change. It is worth noting that many more colleagues than was the case 15 years ago have staked at least part of their professional reputations on work related to preparation program development and reform.

Finally, it is possible that shifting norms in universities in general and in colleges of education in particular may be responsible for some of the increased attention to program reform. Specifically, at least two forces operating in education schools may be directing, or at least facilitating, program improvement. The first is the increased emphasis "on enhancing the quality of instruction [in] most colleges and universities" (McCarthy & Kuh, 1997, p. 245). The second is the demand by many colleges of education that meaningful connections to practice be established and nurtured. Although sometimes offset by other forces (e.g., the press for research respectability), these two dynamics may be helping to energize efforts to strengthen preparation programs in the area of educational leadership.

A Reforging of the Technical Core: Alterations in the Program Content and Instruction

On the instructional front, a renewed interest in teaching is embedded in the preparation reform narrative. There is evidence of an increase in the use of technology in instruction—in redefining the classroom (e.g., distance learning), in classroom activities (e.g., teaching simulations), and in building working relationships with students outside the class (e.g., e-mail communications). There appears to be greater stress on applied approaches and relevant materials in general and on the additional use of problem- and case-based materials specifically. The emergent cognitive perspectives that are helping to redefine learning seem to be working their way into instructional designs in leadership-preparation programs.

A number of issues in the area of curriculum stand out. To begin with, there is greater interest on matters of teaching and learning, including connections between principals' actions and the core technology. Ethics and values are featured in newly designed preparation programs, course work related to the normative dimensions of educational leadership. Closely connected to the growing interest in values is an expanded concern for the social and cultural influences shaping schooling, what I referred to earlier as the social context of education. A theme that cuts across both of these areas—values and social context—is heightened attention to issues of diversity, race, and gender. Closely related to this last focus, programs for preparing school leaders are devoting more attention to topics related to underserved children and their families, especially to the equity agenda. There is some movement from the discipline-based courses that dominated preparation programs throughout the theory era of the profession. Finally, approaches to inculcating habits of reflection and critical analysis are finding life in preparation programs as we push into the 21st century.

A Reunification of the Profession: Reconnecting the Practice and Academic Arms of the Profession

A central strand in the preparation reform tapestry illuminates efforts to reweave the somewhat tattered fabric that represents the profession of school administration. Although the practice and academic spheres of the profession have been estranged for nearly 50 years, preparation programs are being redesigned to repair that gash. These endeavors are of two types: stronger field-based elements in preparation programs and more robust linkages between university faculty and district- and school-based administrators. On the first topic, preparation programs feature the use of practice-anchored materials to a much greater extent than had been the norm in earlier times. There has been a revitalization of the internship. We also see more attention to related clinical activities—shadowing, interviewing administrators, or working with practitioners on projects, for example. In general, reforging content has surfaced an underlying dynamic for redirecting energy toward the practice aspects of school leadership.

On the second topic, university-field connections, a number of trends are visible. The most evident is an enhanced emphasis on forging partnerships in preparation programs between university-based and school-based educators, including the legitimization of practitioner-based advisory groups to help inform preparation program design and content. Another piece of the university-field matrix underscores the rejuvenation of adjunct and clinical faculty roles.

Cracks in the Monopoly Structure of Delivery: Alternative Preparation Models

During its short history, formal preparation for the role of school leader has been the purview of universities, with the imprimatur of state government agencies. Under the onslaught of critical analysis and the renewed interest in the power of markets described in the second section, the monopolistic position of universities has come under attack (Murphy & Hawley, 2003). It is increasingly being asserted that preparation might occur more productively in venues other than universities and be provided more effectively by other agents than faculty members in departments of educational leadership.

In response to these forces, alternative pathways to the role of formal school leader are emerging, again with the warrant of the state. New pathways feature providers not historically associated with the preparation of school administrators. In Table 1, I list six alternative models of preparation, roughly in degree of aggressiveness in opening up the preparation function.

Under alternative *university models*, the preparation function remains in institutions of higher education but it is no longer restricted to colleges of education, or, if it is so restricted, departments other than school leadership are brought into the picture. For example, focusing on the former scenario, New Jersey allows anyone with a degree in administration (e.g., business administration, public administration) to become a school leader. Under the latter scenario, one could become a school administrator with a degree in psychology or curriculum and instruction, for example.

Professional models transfer responsibility for preparation from universities to professional associations. For example, professional groups in California, Massachusetts, and New Jersey are all in the business of preparing newly minted school leaders. In New Jersey, the New Jersey Principals and Supervisors Association's Expedited Certification for Education Leadership (EXCEL) programs employ practice-based educators to prepare teachers to become certified to be school administrators. *District models*, in turn, make the employer the prime actor in the preparation drama, as is the case in Houston and other districts through the country, especially large-city school systems.

Table 1.　Alternative Models for Preparing School Leaders

Traditional Model
　　Institutes of Higher Learning—Departments of School Administration

Alternative Models
　　University Models—Other Colleges than Education
　　　　　　　　　　　—Other Departments in Colleges of Education
　　Professional Models (New Jersey EXCEL Program)
　　Districts Models (Houston)
　　Entrepreneurial Models (New Leaders for New Schools)
　　Private Models (Canter and Associates)
　　Experiential Models (Waivers for superintendents without educational backgrounds)

Entrepreneurial models combine the insights of creative individuals outside the university and the resources of committed reformers, almost always philanthropic foundations. The best-known examples here are Dennis Litkey and his Big Picture Company with its school-based, mentoring model of preparation and Jon Schnur and Monique Burns and the New Leaders for New Schools program to prepare nontraditional actors as school administrators for urban school systems.

The efforts of for-profit firms fall into the category of *private models*. The most extensive and visible example here is the Leadership for Learning master's program developed by Canter and Associates, which it developed in partnership with the American Association of School Administrators. *Experiential models* permit potential administrators to substitute work experience for course work. Although to date almost all initiatives in this area have been ad hoc (e.g., a waiver to certification regulations), it is likely that the profession will see more systematic initiatives to allow work experience to substitute for formal preparation in the future.

I close this discussion on alternative preparation with a few notes to deepen the narrative. To begin, it is important to remember that state-level policy is generally the linchpin here, either reinforcing or deconstructing university control in the area of administrator preparation. Second, hybrid models are often visible on the alternative pathway landscape. For example, as noted above, Canter and Associates, a for-profit company, is working in partnership with the American Association of School Administrators, a professional association. In a similar vein, district models (e.g., Houston) and professional models (e.g., Massachusetts) often work with universities. And New Leaders for New Schools and the Big Picture Company, both entrepreneurial models, work with districts and universities, respectively. Third, it is instructive to remember that "alternative" does not mean "better." Novelty is certainly not a significant criterion for judging the usefulness of reform initiatives. And neither, for that matter, is the venue of delivery. Indeed, initial analyses of these alternative models suggest that while they do open up the supply side of the choice equation, they also share a good deal of common ground with university-based programs, especially those engaged in their own reform efforts. Fourth, as I discuss later, there is very little empirical evidence on these alternative preparation efforts. Impact data, in particular, are nearly conspicuous by their absence. Fifth, as my work on privatization reveals (Murphy, 1996, 1999c; Murphy & Shiffman, 2002; Murphy et al., 1998), the road between deregulation and enhanced outcomes is littered with contradictory ideological claims and inconsistent empirical conclusions, both in the larger sphere of government services and in the field of education.

7

An Agenda for Research and Action

In the final two chapters of this review on preparation programs, I address two tasks. First, I review findings about the nature of research on the preparatory function. Second, based upon that data, as well as all the information presented in the narrative to this point, I outline an agenda for strengthening research on preparation programs.

A NOTE ON RESEARCH
IN SCHOOL ADMINISTRATION IN GENERAL

Because research on preparation programs is a subset of empirical work on school administration, it is instructive to provide a short synopsis of this more general topic, that is, to note findings about the state of research in school administration writ large, especially on issues of methodology. This larger question assumes added significance when it is recalled that there is only one existing review on the research about preparation programs. Over the past half century, leading figures in the profession have turned their analytic lenses on this inquiry, either directly (e.g., Boyan, 1981; Bridges, 1982; Campbell, 1979; Erickson, 1967, 1979; Lipham, 1964; McNamara, 1978; Miskel & Sandlin, 1981) or indirectly, for example, through explorations of the work of faculty in educational leadership (see Campbell, 1981; Campbell & Newell, 1973; McCarthy et al., 1988; McCarthy & Kuh, 1997), through examination of activities in preparation

JOLIET JUNIOR COLLEGE
JOLIET, IL 60431

programs (see Griffiths et al., 1988b; Silver & Spuck, 1978), or through treatments of the historical development of the profession (see Campbell et al., 1987; Culbertson, 1995; Murphy, 1992). As a consequence, concerns about research in education leadership have "continued since Griffiths (1959) first sounded the alarm 40 years ago" (Tschannen-Moran et al., 2000, p. 380). Throughout that time, "scholars and practitioners alike have claimed that research on educational administration is lacking" (Ogawa, Goldring, & Conley, 2000, p. 340). Reviewers have unearthed "problems in the quality and utility of research in education administration" (Pounder, 2000, p. 465), as well as with the quantity. Key findings that emerge from analyses of research in educational administration are noted as follows.

Quantity

Although the volume of research increased during the last half of the 20th century, concerns about the quantity of research in school administration have not abated. Immegart (1990) made this point cogently at the macro level when he characterized "the relatively weak level and extent of scholarship evident in the field generally" (p. 5). Riehl and her colleagues (2000) arrived at a similar conclusion in the recent report of the Division A Task Force on Research and Inquiry in Educational Administration. They assert that "in contrast with the growing body of teacher research, there is little evidence of similar growth within educational administration" (p. 399), a point that Firestone and Riehl (2003) reinforce in their prospectus to the proposed volume of the task force's work: "Research on educational leadership may have had such limited impact because so little of it has actually been done" (p. 1).

Faculty Engagement

Closely connected to the issue of quantity is the breadth and depth of faculty involvement in the research domain of the profession. As I discussed in my critique of the delivery system in preparation programs, analysts investigating the topic of breadth have concluded that only "a small number of those in the field of educational administration actively engage in scholarly activities" (Immegart, 1990, p. 11), or "contribute systematically and regularly to the scholarly body . . . of literature" (Boyan, 1981, p. 7). In 1965, "Hills found that 53% of his sample of professors devoted 'no time whatsoever' to research" (Miskel, 1988, p. 16). In his review of scholarship in *Educational Administration Quarterly* in 1979, Campbell found that 82% of the articles in the first 14 volumes were penned by authors in only 26 institutions. Thus, throughout the history of school administration, "most [professors] were occupied with a range of activities that precluded serious and sustained scholarship" (Campbell et al., 1987, p. 184). The profession has depended on "the willing or the driven few to participate in scholarly activities" (Immegart, 1990, p. 5).

On the issue of depth, most research-active professors continue to be able to devote only a small portion of their work portfolios to research endeavors —14.4% according to McCarthy and Kuh (1997). And although that proportion is on the rise (McCarthy & Kuh, 1997), even today "it seems that faculty members in educational administration generally lack strong orientations and commitments to research or scholarship" (Miskel, 1988, p. 16).

A related topic of interest is the significant extent to which the research base in educational administration is a product of doctoral dissertations, a phenomenon that also has important ramifications for issues of quality. Analysts across the decades have detected two interconnected trends in this regard: (a) "most of the research on educational administration is done by graduate students" (Immegart, 1977, p. 302) and (b) "the dissertation in educational administration [is] the primary method of creating knowledge in the field" (Miskel, 1988, p. 23).

Focus of Inquiry

Reviewers have applied two lines of analysis to the topic of research focus in school administration. To begin with, colleagues have provided a series of explorations about the topics of interest embedded in studies. These reviews portray the research terrain, noting areas of interest, both established and emerging, and unearthing topics that are, from the perspectives of the reviewers, insufficiently investigated. For example, in an early review of the state of research in school administration, Lipham (1964) examined three "refreshing new directions[s]: increased emphasis on organizational change, analysis of interpersonal perception, and renewed interest in the administrative process" (p. 435). Examples of gaps in the research agenda are also prevalent. Erickson (1979) reported a near absence of attention to issues of educational productivity and the study of organizational outcomes. Bridges (1982) described the anemic state of affairs in regard to research on the superintendency. And Murphy (1992) noted that research on the linkages between school administration and learning was conspicuous by its absence.

A second line of investigation on the focus of empirical endeavors attends to the coherence and cumulative nature of research. The chronicle constructed over time on this issue is disheartening. The central thread of the storyline is one that might at best be characterized as ad hoc (Pounder, 2000), or less charitably as "faddish" (Firestone & Riehl, 2003, p. 1). In the mid-1970s, Immegart (1977) reported that research in educational administration "tend[ed] to follow 'hot' topics, social concerns, particular concepts, or 'practical presses of the time'" (p. 316). He found that there were "really no significant programmatic efforts in the study of educational administration" (p. 317). In their reviews in the next decade, both Boyan (1981) and Bridges (1982) arrived at the same end point, discerning that "research problems are treated in an ad hoc rather than programmatic fashion" (Bridges, 1982, p. 13). By the turn of the century, although the language used to describe the findings was more scientific in tone, the central theme of the research narrative was largely unaltered. For example, analysts on the Division A Task Force on Research and Inquiry in Educational Administration concluded "that there was not enough sustained, disciplined, focused empirical inquiry and that there was a tendency to move from one interesting idea or concept to the next without serious research accumulating" (Tschannen-Moran et al., 2000, p. 381). The consequence of this intermittent, shifting, and ad hoc approach to research in the profession—"the fact that there is little cumulative building of knowledge in the field" (Campbell, 1979, p. 10)—has been illuminated by nearly every analysis of the state of research in school administration: "the quality and ultimately the utility of our research efforts . . . are compromised" (Pounder, 2000, p. 466) and we are left with a "shallow pool of research evidence on any given area of focus" (p. 466).

Methodological Approaches

Over the years, scholars have invested considerable time exposing the methodological scaffolding supporting research studies in school administration. They have also conducted assessments of the quality of the methods employed. In terms of design, reviewers have consistently noted "a pervasive use of survey methods" (Miskel & Sandlin, 1981, p. 1). Indeed, Bridges (1982) portrays survey research design as "the darling of scholars who study school administration" (p. 15). Not surprisingly, the use of questionnaires has dominated data collection in the profession (Miskel & Sandlin, 1981). Description rather than explanation holds the high ground and univariate analysis predominates.

Reviewers consistently find ample room for improvement across the methodological landscape of studies in school administration. In general, even when the focus is on the top academic journals (Miskel & Sandlin, 1981), they detect "weak design, treatment, and analysis" (Boyan, 1981, p. 9). They also perceive that over time "improvements have been uneven and modest" (Miskel & Sandlin, 1981, p. 17).

Impact

Beginning with the onset of the theory movement in school administration, scholars have been interested in locating and describing the effect of research on the profession, especially on the knowledge structure and on administrative practice. On the first issue, the Division A Task Force on Research and Inquiry in Educational Administration maintains that research on school leadership has generated few robust conclusions (Firestone & Riehl, 2003). Likewise, employing the "influence on practice" standard, scholars arrive at a similar endgame (Erickson, 1977; Murphy & Vriesenga, 2004), concluding that "analysis yields little evidence that research and inquiry have had any substantial impact on practice" (Immegart, 1977, p. 317): "In short there is no compelling evidence to suggest that a major theoretical issue or practical problem relating to school administrators has been resolved by those toiling in the intellectual vineyards since 1967" (Bridges, 1982, p. 25).

Summary

Culbertson (1995) reports in his volume on the history of the early decades of UCEA that there is disagreement about whether the quantity of research in school administration increased from the start of the theory movement circa 1950. And to be sure, gains are discernable, in the number of professors engaging in research and the amount of their work portfolios devoted to scholarship, in the variety of methods brought to bear on questions, in the sophistication of analytic lenses employed in studies, and so forth. Not withstanding this conclusion, the overall portrait of research in the field is considerably bleaker than most would prefer.

FINDINGS ABOUT RESEARCH AND PREPARATION PROGRAMS

As I noted, although there is a considerable body of writing on the preparatory function in school administration, there is only one review of empirical work on preparation. That investigation was undertaken by Murphy and Vriesenga (2004). The seven central findings from that analysis of research published in the leading journals in school administration—*EAQ*, *JEA*, *JSL*, *Planning and Changing*—are sketched out below.

1. *There is not an overabundance of scholarship in the area of administrator preparation.* At least when we focus on the leading journals in school leadership, it is clear that descriptions and analyses of preparation programs do not occupy much space in these outlets. Only 8% of the 2000-plus articles in these journals from 1975 to 2002 dealt with preservice training programs. Given the applied nature of the profession and the centrality of preparatory activities to departments of educational leadership, the fact that serious academic work on preservice training remains a minor element in the school administration scholarship mosaic is as surprising as it is disappointing.

2. *Work in entire domains of administrator preparation is conspicuous by its absence.* Although in no area of administrator preparation is there a surfeit of work, at least on some topics an initial body of literature is developing. On the other hand, very little study has been directed toward entire sections of the preparatory landscape. Specifically, we know very little about issues ranging from how we recruit and select students, instruct them in our programs, and monitor and assess their progress. Organizational life inside programs is hardly touched upon in the research literature. We also learn remarkably little from the journals

about the faculty members who develop and operate these programs. In particular, there is almost no empirical evidence on the education of those who educate prospective school leaders.

3. *The contours of school leadership are only weakly shaped by empirical evidence on preparation programs.* Slightly less than 3% [56] of the 2000-plus articles published between 1975 and 2002 in the leading journals in our field are empirically anchored investigations on administrator preparation. Although we seem to know about this topic, as evidenced in the abundance of writing and professing in the area, very little of our understanding has been forged on the empirical anvil. While it is appropriate for the field to incorporate multiple ways of knowing about the preparation experience, the very limited attention devoted to empirical studies remains a serious problem.

4. *The amount of scholarship devoted to administrator preparation is expanding.* Between 1975 and 1990, approximately 3% of the articles in the leading journals addressed administrator preservice training. Since that time, more than 11 percent of the articles have attended to training issues. During the earlier time period, less than 1% of journal space was devoted to empirical work on preparation programs. Since 1990, nearly 4% of the articles in the four leading journals in our field have been given over to empirical studies of administrator preservice training. Concomitantly, individual faculty have become scholars of specific areas within preparation programs, conducting critical and empirical investigations on the topic at hand (see, for example, the extended work of Barnett, Basom, Yerkes, and Norris [2000] in the area of student cohorts, as well as that of Kochan and Twale, 1998, Daresh, on clinical work; and McCarthy and her research team, 1988 and 1997, on faculty issues).

5. *The methodological scaffolding supporting empirical studies has been expanded, yet it is not clear that quality has been greatly enhanced.* When one steps back and examines the full landscape of empirical work on preparation programs, it is obvious that the terrain is populated not only more densely but also by a greater variety of studies than has been the case in the field of school leadership in general in the past. In particular, incipient efforts into blended methods and the mushrooming use of naturalistic designs have significantly

expanded the assortment of studies in the preparation area. Concomitantly, the importation of an entire new set of analytic strategies
has enriched the architectural design undergirding preparation
programs.

Although in many ways the expansion of the methods portfolio
has strengthened the study of the preparatory function (e.g., it has
helped us see issues from multiple angles and sometimes more
deeply as well), it has not made a large dent in overcoming many of
the deficiencies noted in the introductory part of this section. In particular, the expanded portfolio has not helped produce much traction
on the following issues: the ad hoc nature of the work; an overreliance on cross-sectional investigations; the use of limited samples;
inadequately developed (or at least described) analytic frames; and
a lack of depth, or a heavy focus on the surface issues, of topics under investigation.

6. *Dissertation work comprises a small but not insignificant proportion of published research.* As discussed at the beginning of this
section, reviewers of research in school administration in general
have long noted the prominent place that doctoral students occupy
in building the knowledge base in the profession. However, when
the lens is directed on published articles focusing on administrator
preparation in refereed journals, that conclusion is muted. Of the
56 empirical studies published in the leading journals over the past
quarter century, only three can be traced directly to a dissertation.
When the names of the authors of these 56 pieces were matched
with dissertations, seven additional articles that could be coupled
to dissertation research were located—for a total of 18%. In addition, four dissertations that were loosely linked to the content of an
article published in one of the leading journals in school administration were found.

7. *There is almost no evidence of external support for empirical research on preparation programs.* For the 56 empirical studies, there
is either direct or indirect reference to external funding in only three,
and two of these represent very limited support. It appears that professors who engage in research on preparation programs continue to

do so out of their back pockets, relying on (a) the good will of current and recent graduates to complete surveys or sit for interviews and (b) residual documents associated with preparation programs (e.g., admissions records). It is difficult to see how the profession can gain much leverage on developing systematic and programmatic work on preparation without additional support.

8

Strengthening Scholarship and Research on the Preparatory Function

SOME GENERAL IDEAS

A central recommendation of this review is that research on preparation be highlighted more fully in the profession. In this section, I suggest some general ideas that move us in that direction, ideas that mirror proven strategies in the other domains of school leadership and in the area of preservice preparation in such related fields as teaching.

I believe that a commission report that sets the agenda for research on preparation would provide a much-needed platform for action. Commissioned work could fall to either a group that represents the profession, such as the National Policy Board for Educational Administration, or to highly visible extant operational initiative, such as the National Commission on the Advancement of Educational Leadership Preparation. What I envision here is a blueprint for action based on a comprehensive review of the preparation domain. I would hope that the analyses and suggestions contained in this report would find their way into the mix of ideas such a commission would generate.

I also believe that a *Handbook of Research on Administrator Preparation* that parallels work undertaken in teacher education could make a major contribution to strengthening research on preservice preparation. The first volume in what I hope would be a periodic series might be devoted as much to conducting and reporting on initial studies as it is to reviewing existing research. As was the case with the commission activity discussed above, a central dimension of the individual chapters and the summary material would be the crafting of the broad outlines for improving research in this underinvestigated sphere of educational leadership. It also seems reasonable to suggest that a journal be created that is dedicated to scholarship and research on the education of school leaders, especially to reviews of research and to empirical investigations. Teacher development has been advantaged by the presence of a number of journals dedicated to the education of teachers, including the *Journal of Teacher Education* (which has been publishing useful material for over half a century), *Teaching and Teacher Education*, and *Teacher Education Quarterly*. Given the importance of preparation to the profession, a journal published under the aegis of the University Council for Educational Administration and/or the National Council of Professors of Educational Administration would seem appropriate. Concomitantly, I maintain that the major professional organizations in school administration could be more forceful in underscoring the place of scholarship in preservice education. I believe that our leaders should designate and sustain "leadership preparation" as one of the program areas in the call for proposals for Division A of AERA. I also suggest that regular conferences on leadership preparation, either in conjunction with NCPEA or UCEA or as freestanding events, be planned.

A TARGETED AGENDA

I begin here with two observations that, although obvious by this point in my review, need to be recorded. First, "research on educational leadership preparation programs, faculty members, and students is needed to inform deliberations about how to better prepare school leaders" (McCarthy, 1999, p. 135). Second, there simply is not much research on the preparatory function in school administration and the research we do have does not seem to be sufficiently powerful to drive change efforts. As Forsyth and Willower (1999) reported in their influential *Handbook* article, "Most of the scholarly writing in preparation programs consists of broad treatments that connect reform to issues in education or society or analysis of particular reforms, often critical of the status quo and supportive of specific changes, seen as improvements" (p. 18). And as Murphy and Vriesenga (2004) recently concluded, attempting to form a coherent understanding of the preparation function in school administration is a bit like trying to create a unified artistic product by aggregating the efforts of impoverished artists working alone across a half dozen or so different forms of expression. So the question resurfaces: Where might we begin the work to deepen our understanding of the education of school administrators and to strengthen the preparatory programs that train future school leaders? Below I outline seven specific areas where I believe additional research could be especially beneficial in meeting these two objectives.

1. *Research on the landscape of preparation.* It is generally a wise idea to plan change based on a firm foundation of the current situation. Unfortunately, such knowledge is in very short supply in the area of administrator preparation. Not since the hallmark UCEA studies conducted by Silver (1978a, 1978b) and Silver and Spuck (1978) in the mid-1970s has the field undertaken a comprehensive, large-scale investigation of the preparatory function in school administration. I suggest that it is past time to update and replicate this landmark research effort. Equally important, in the same way that the profession has approached examination of the professoriate (Campbell & Newell, 1973; McCarthy et al., 1988; McCarthy & Kuh, 1997), this comprehensive study of preparation should be conducted on a regular basis so that we can track changes afoot in the education of school leaders across time.

2. *Research on the reform agenda of the last 15 years.* The third era of ferment in school administration described in the first section above has resulted in the development of numerous ideas that, we are told, are being woven together to create a new preparation tapestry (Hart & Pounder, 1999; Murphy, 1999b, 1999a; Murphy & Forsyth, 1999). Yet there has been remarkably little empirical work on these reform issues and "few extensive studies of the impacts of these reforms exist" (Hart & Pounder, 1999, p. 146). More importantly, as McCarthy (1999) observes, "there is meager research relating recent . . . innovations in preparation programs to administrative success or evaluating administrators' use of knowledge gained in preparation programs" (p. 134).

3. *Research on effective preparation programs.* Given the long history in education of constructing improvement designs from studies of

effective operations (e.g., effective schools, effective special programs for youngsters, effective curricular programs), it is interesting that studies of highly productive preparation programs should be nearly nonexistent (see Murphy, 1993; Jackson & Kelley, 2002). Certainly part of the explanation centers on difficulties in developing conceptions of productive programs and in marshaling evidence of effectiveness. Still, given the prevalence and acceptance of "reputation" as a measure of effectiveness in initial work in other domains (see, for example, Fisher and Adler, 1999, in the area of effective reading programs), the research gap here is disheartening.

4. *Research on alternative designs for preparation.* As discussed in earlier sections, for much of the past 15 years, considerable energy has been invested in bringing market forces to systems of education throughout the United States, to the PK–12 system and to colleges of education. At the university level, this has meant that the protective walls of monopoly surrounding higher-education institutions have been breached. More concretely, it has led to the enfranchisement of alternative providers for the education of school administrators. Districts (e.g., Houston), professional associations (e.g., the New Jersey Principals and Supervisors Association), policy entrepreneurs (e.g., the Broad Foundation), and private firms (e.g., Sylvan Learning Corporation) have all begun to carve off pieces of program preparation for themselves. While we are bombarded with information about the expected benefits of these new arrangements, we know very little about them empirically. I am aware of no study that lays out in a comprehensive manner a description of these alternative designs—a picture of what the changing preparatory terrain looks like. Consequently, we know very little about the designs of these alternative models. And, of course, almost no evidence has been accumulated to support or refute claims made by advocates and opponents for shifting the locus of control over the preparation function away from universities. While the theory in action that powers the development of alternative designs enjoys a good deal of allure, researchers should hold two cautions in mind as investigations in this area take shape. First, nonuniversity providers held the keys to the preparation function, at least for teachers, for a good part of our history. The reasons university-anchored alternatives to district-

based preparation began to dominate training have not disappeared. Or stated more starkly, to date "there appears to be little, if any, evidence that suggests that we can develop good schools for all America's children by disconnecting the generation of principals and superintendents from university-based programs" (Grogan & Andrews, 2002, p. 249). Second, students of school improvement remind us that the belief that a change in the venue of delivery in and of itself will produce different outcomes is empirically nonsupportable (Murphy, 1991b; Murphy & Beck, 1995).

5. *Research on program outcomes.* In my earlier compilation of concerns about preparation program in school administration, I documented that for the past 60 years, analysts have pointed out that the profession is characterized by a dearth of research on the outcomes of preparation programs. Worse yet, until quite recently, the field has appeared to be genetically incapable of gaining traction on this matter.

Recent work, however, has begun to conceptualize research designs to examine the effectiveness of preparation programs (see Glasman et al., 2002; Orr & Kottkamp, 2003). According to these scholars, on a continuum of depth, evaluation efforts fall into one of five dimensions:

a. participant satisfaction with the program and its component elements,
b. knowledge and skill acquisition,
c. use of skills and knowledge,
d. organizational impact, and
e. performance of youngsters in the school in which a program graduate is working.

An examination of the quite limited empirical work on program evaluation and/or program effectiveness reveals that in nearly 80% of the published studies, the focus is on the process elements or the internal components of the training program (e.g., the curriculum taught or the instructional strategies employed). Almost always, assessments of these elements rely upon the perceptions of current or former students in the program. In general (nonuniversity-specific) studies, these evaluations ask students to assess program quality by noting areas that were done well or poorly and by pointing out topics and domains that received insufficient attention in their training programs. In evaluations of specific university programs, current and/or recently graduated students are required to judge (a) the degree to which program goals were met, (b) the extent to which program elements were valuable, and/or (c) self-perceived growth. Only a very few studies have attempted to move beyond the first level on the assessment continuum, that is to design and execute more robust investigations. There are no research articles in the leading journals in the field over the past quarter century that directly assess the skills and knowledge gained in preparation programs; nor do any articles measure changes in the performance of students in schools of program graduates (Murphy & Vriesenga, 2004).

On the upside, colleagues who have completed existing studies have pointed us in the right direction. They have also driven some important foundational pillars on which the next generation of work in this long-neglected area can build. These are hardly minor accomplishments. At the same time, my review here illuminates problems that resurface throughout this analysis. Existing studies represent an oasis rather than a fertile field of knowledge. Work here, as elsewhere, remains ad hoc in nature. I also see the tendency for studies to pick off the low-hanging fruit; inquiry around the more difficult, more complex, yet ultimately more meaningful questions is largely missing. Pursuing this avenue, by design, overvalues the perceptions of program participants vis-à-vis the insights of others who work with graduates of preparation programs, as well as other forms of, perhaps, more compelling evidence. Thus, why colleagues have illuminated the path ahead, research to date does not take us much beyond the starting point.

6. *Research on the context of preparation programs.* To date, scholars attending to the profession of school administration have lavished almost all of their ink on the reform churn inside the field, for example, the struggle over an appropriate knowledge base for preparation programs (see Donmoyer, 1999; Forsyth & Murphy, 1999; Murphy, 1999d). At the same time, they have devoted remarkably little energy to conceptualizing and studying the context that envelops the preparatory function. This is a costly omission at any time. It is especially problematic in periods when environments are

in flux. My analysis leads me to conclude that we are experiencing a good deal of contextual seismic activity at the current time. For example, as is the case in PK–12 education (Murphy, 1990b), states are exerting unprecedented influence over what historically has been a somewhat autonomous sphere of activity. At the same time, policy entrepreneurs (e.g., the foundation community) are throwing considerable new energy into the environment surrounding the administrative preparatory function. The points for us here are similar to those introduced elsewhere in this narrative. First, we lack research that provides a portrait of the shifting context in which preparation activity is unfolding. Second, we have almost no research on how this context is influencing the scope and texture of the preparatory function in school administration.

7. *Longitudinal and comprehensive research on specific domains of administration preparation.* In their recent review of research on teacher preparation, Wilson and her colleagues (2001) concluded that in-depth investigations of "particular components of teacher education" (p. 35) should be an essential element in the future research agenda on the education of school teachers. Based on my review of the literature here, I reach a similar conclusion for school administration. By way of illustration, I describe the research terrain on four "components" of preparation and offer suggestions about how to nurture the growth of a lusher landscape.

Clinical Work

Between 1978 and 2002, five empirical articles on clinical work were published in the four leading refereed journals in school administration, none by the same researcher(s). One investigation provided a descriptive overview of field-based experiences in selected, UCEA-based programs. The other four all attended to various aspects of the internship: a tool for identifying mentors, an analysis of what should be included in an internship experience, a description of activities found in internships, with assessments of the quality of those components, and an investigation of the impact of the internship experience on learners and mentors. A few observations here merit notice. To begin with, to reinforce a central theme of this analysis, there simply are too few empirical studies to say much about the internship with any degree of confidence. Given the centrality of the internship to the education process in applied fields and its prominent position in the professional accreditation process (e.g., NCATE), this is troublesome. It is also noteworthy that the larger picture of clinical work across preparation programs is rarely illuminated. In particular, the empirical literature on clinical work provides no insights on how field-based work is woven into and across learning experiences throughout training programs. Given the struggle to scaffold preparation programs in general and classes in particular onto problems of practice rather than academic disciplines, the study of field-based work needs considerably more attention than it has received over the past century.

Students

The body of work here does a reasonable job of marking key dimensions of the student domain of the preparation landscape but does very little to populate the terrain. For example, for nearly half a century critics have bemoaned the state of recruitment and selection in preparation programs (for example, in the 1950s, see Hall and McIntyre, 1957; in the 1960s, AASA, 1960; in the 1970s, Tyack and Cummings, 1977; in the 1980s, AACTE, 1988; in the 1990s, Jacobson, 1990; and in the current decade, Creighton, 2002). Yet the quite limited body of empirical knowledge we have does little to help us gain purchase on the problem. With the exception of studies on cohorts, there are practically no empirical investigations of students inside preparation programs. Important topics, such as the assessment of students, almost never appear on the research radar screen, at least as reflected in the profession's key journals. In general, "students tend to be routinely overlooked" (McCarthy, 1999, p. 134).

Program Structure and Collaborative Work

Program structure refers to the organization dimensions of how preservice training systems are constructed and delivered, for example, whether a program is offered on campus or in a school district, whether it is taught in a traditional format or online. From the assortment of topics that occupy this domain, only the use of cohorts has received any sustained empirical attention in the leading journals of the profession. In a similar fashion, although the general publication literature and the nonempirical scholarship in the leading journals have attended at least somewhat to the matter of collaboration in the development, delivery, and oversight of preparation programs, that limited interest does not extend to empirical studies. Only one study in the leading journals in school administration over the past quarter century looked empirically at collaboration (see Kochan & Twale, 1998).

Instruction and Curriculum

Instruction in graduate preparation programs in school leadership is only very lightly studied, with only five empirical pieces in the four leading academic journals in the field being devoted to teaching over the past quarter century. Three hot topics—problem-based learning, action research, and experience-based instruction—anchor four of the five pieces. The major vault in the curricular warehouse contains information about what is, and more often what is not, being done in particular curricular domains, with one eye focused on improving the situation. Nonetheless, it would take leap of faith to draw many conclusions from this limited body of empirical research on curriculum in preparation programs. Indeed, from the extant research, we know little about the traditional curricular domains of preparation programs (e.g., finance, personnel), nor are we provided with much knowledge about the shape of curriculum in a post-theory era, where issues around learning and teaching and community are reshaping the profession.

Some Concluding Comments

Looking across these recommendations, it seems to me that we would do well to focus considerable energy on the two big-picture ideas. First, we need to know who we are and what we are doing in the area of leadership preparation. We need to do for preparation what Campbell and Newell (1973) and McCarthy and her colleagues (1988, 1997) have done for the professoriate. We need a comprehensive analysis of the state of the field and we need that analysis to reoccur at regular intervals so we can see how and why the preparation function is developing. UCEA through the efforts of Silver (1978a, 1978b) and Silver and Spuck (1978) laid the groundwork for us a quarter century ago. It is more than desirable that we follow up on that seminal initiative. It would provide an excellent background and useful roadmaps for the work that needs to be engaged. Second, the fragmentary and decentralized approach we have been following in our efforts to strengthen leadership preparation (and to conduct research in school administration, for that matter) has proven itself to be fairly barren. We need to come together as a profession to establish a collective agenda around the training and education function. We need to underscore the importance of a small number of important issues that we collectively agree to attack with sufficient force and over a long enough period of time to ensure the likelihood of garnering positive results. To be sure, there are problems associated with this path of action, especially those connected to the need for strong center of action. It seems—to me, at least—that to fail to move in this direction almost guarantees more of the same, individual efforts that do not add up to much and that provide illusionary gains at best.

9

Responses

PREPARING NEW LEADERS FOR THE "NEW ECONOMY"

Gary L. Anderson
New York University

The other day I visited an administrative intern at a high school on New York's Lower East Side. I had directed a program at this school in 1981, and I was curious as to how it had changed. I realized things were different as I made my way through a cluster of seven armed NYPD uniformed police officers chatting inside the lobby. These were clearly not youth workers or detectives, but rather beat cops who seemed to me to be wildly out of place in this context. After signing in and receiving my identity sticker, I made my way to the metal detector, where surly security agents made airport security feel downright uplifting. I could not help but feel sorry for the students who had to experience this humiliation on a daily basis. So much for building trust.

I greeted the principal and mentioned how much the school had changed since I had been there in the early '80s. I was surprised at his candor as he indicated that post-Columbine and post-9/11 schools had become armed camps. We discussed an outstanding Bronx principal who just a few days earlier had been arrested along with a student for trying to handle a discipline incident in his own school. Although he and I both recognized that safety needed to be a top priority in urban schools, he expressed his concern that not only were businessmen and politicians now making educational decisions but that principals couldn't even handle their own discipline problems. He said that the cops often behaved inappropriately with the kids, sometimes flirting with the girls, making students more angry and unruly when they arrived to class. He said that the metal detectors meant that kids sometimes waited 45 minutes in the rain or snow to get into the building, adding to the humiliation of the whole process and leading to increased tardiness and truancy. He said he had never felt so little autonomy over his professional life.

Anyone who spends even a little time in low-income urban and rural schools must realize how out of touch research in the field of educational administration is with the reality of school life today. There are transformations occurring in our educational system that useful but timid theories of "distributed leadership," "learning organizations," and "parent involvement" do not come close to addressing. In an age of a costly American empire and an underfunded, nonmilitary public sector, low-income schools are embattled fortresses that offer students few opportunities besides the military, prison, or jobs in the low-wage service sector—opportunities that will add them to the ranks of a new and growing class in America: the working poor.

In *Preparing School Leaders: Defining a Research and Action Agenda*, Joe Murphy documents the present state of research in educational administration, presenting literature focused on organizations and leadership within organizations. His characterization of the literature in the field is largely depressingly correct, although there is movement around the edges that focuses on what is generally referred to as "social justice" issues, a topic that is far more substantial than is suggested by his review.

Murphy valiantly tries to draw some conclusions and provide recommendations from the handful of largely anecdotal studies of administrator preparation programs. While acknowledging the futility of the task, he does document a rising interest in administrator preparation evidenced by new AERA Special Interest Groups and a small but growing number of journal articles and UCEA and NPCEA conference presentations. This is good news, but I will argue here that a reconceptualization of administrator preparation is needed that goes far beyond current research in the field on educational leadership and administrator preparation. This reconceptualization requires both a thoroughgoing shift in how we understand (a) the theory-practice relationship and the kinds of research that might address it, (b) the preparation of reflective leaders that can *problematize* as well as *problem solve*, and (c) the relationship of what goes on in schools with broader social, cultural, and economic shifts that are occurring both globally and nationally. I am not calling for a new theory movement that shifts from behavioral science theories to socioeconomic theories—however "critical"—disconnected from school life. Rather, I am suggesting that professors of educational administration work closely with practitioners to better understand how the kinds of changes in schools I have described above are entangled in larger geopolitical and economic shifts that are being manifested both under our noses and over our heads. The preparation of administrators also must include conversations about winners and losers in the new economy and how winning and losing is related to ongoing disparities in outcomes by race, gender, class, and sexual orientation.

It is not that Murphy does not attempt to address these larger structural shifts. He does discuss the decline in civil society and the expansion of market forces to replace public service delivery and he seems to see both a reinvigorated market and a return to local democracy as solutions. Markets and local democracy are both revered American institutions that have played significant roles in American society. But while celebrating them, we also should carefully analyze how they have also been used to protect privilege. Uncritical assumptions about markets and local democracy increasingly creep into literature in educational administration (Anderson, 1998). A point made several times by Murphy in different ways is the following: "Most chroniclers of the changing governance structures in schools envision the demise of schooling as a sheltered government monopoly heavily controlled by professionals." It is not clear who "most chroniclers" refers to, but this is the mantra mainly of right-wing think tanks and other neoliberal and libertarian commentators. The notion of a monopoly of professionals in the public sector appears throughout and becomes a major part of Murphy's agenda for the future of preparation programs as he notes, "At the university level, this has meant that the protective walls of monopoly surrounding higher-education institutions have been breached." Among the beneficiaries of breaching this "monopoly," according to Murphy, are "private firms (e.g. Sylvan Learning Corporation)." Sylvan Learning Corporation is, among other things, a for-profit company that Murphy himself has promoted as a university partner for the preparation of school administrators.

Of course, the real monopolies are not in the public sector at all. For instance, we live in a country in which two or three corporations now own the bulk of our media outlets. However, a favorite ploy of privatizers is to shift the notion of monopoly to the public sector, which represents—at least in theory—public will, unlike the corporate sector, which represents a small, elite group of stockholders focused not on a larger public interest, but rather on short-term private profits.

Murphy draws heavily on work—though not much is cited—that sees "at the institutional level, a rebalancing of the equation that adds more weight to market and citizen control while subtracting influence from government and professional actors" (?). Traditionally, citizen or local control is evoked by groups that want to maintain their privileges. The history of America is replete with small elite groups that have used local control or "states' rights" to protect racial, educational, or financial privilege. The combining of citizen control and market forces is a clear case of the antipolitics that is replacing democratic political entities with market-oriented choice schemes, such as vouchers that claim to devolve power to local communities through choice. Although Murphy talks a lot about democracy, it is not clear how he sees democracy operating in a shrinking public sphere. In this age of privately funded think tanks that more effectively disseminate knowledge/ ideology than universities do, one has to learn the code words of the new neoliberal agenda as they seep into our own research.

But let me back up and place this political and economic analysis in perspective. A reconceptualization of administrator preparation will not only require a clearer picture of shifts in the governance of schools and their relationship to the economy, the military, and the juvenal justice system but also a serious discussion of the relationship of research and social theory to the everyday practice of administrators in schools. So rather than start at the level of theory and work down, as academics—especially "critical" ones— tend to do, let's see if we can rethink this relationship of theory to practice.

WORKING THE THEORY-PRACTICE HYPHEN

Citing Boyan (1981), Bridges (1982), Pounder (2000), and others, Murphy argues for a more programmatic research program with greater cumulative building of knowledge in the field. Doctoral programs continue to promote and reward this kind of research, although Pounder, in her response, correctly points out that methodological options have expanded. As a member of the Division A Task Force on Research and Inquiry in Educational Administration, cited frequently by Murphy, I suggested that the way the crisis in research in the field of educational administration was framed was problematic (Anderson & Jones, 2000). As long as we see our research solely as placing another brick in the wall of knowledge about educational administration, we are condemned as a field to fail administrators. Even if we believe the wall of knowledge metaphor is valid, and it may be for some kinds of knowledge, we know that presenting these results of research to practitioners is not a good use of class time. This is a flawed approach to knowledge utilization that has been repeatedly critiqued (Lindblom & Cohen, 1979).

In fact, two out of the four articles published in the special edition of *Educational Administration Quarterly* that contained the task force results called for a reconceptualization of the field around a scholar-practitioner model that honors multiple forms of knowledge generation and utilization. Ironically, Murphy cites the Riehl et al. (2000) article in that issue, using it to support his assertion that there is a paucity of research produced in the field. Citing Immegart (1990), who observed "the relatively weak level and extent of scholarship evident in the field generally (p. 5), he goes on to claim that "Riehl and her colleagues (2000) arrived at a similar conclusion . . . 'in contrast with the growing body of teacher research, there is little evidence of similar growth within educational administration' (p. 399)." Murphy apparently misread "teacher research" as "research on teaching." In reality, the authors of this article are not claiming there is a paucity of research in the field. They are calling for administrators to follow the lead of a robust action research movement called "teacher research" that has become a significant movement among teachers and teacher education programs linked to professional development, learning communities, and knowledge production among teachers. Although this example of Murphy's mischaracterization of literature may seem picky, it illustrates the general dismissal—all too common in the field—of the very epistemology that would allow both professors of educational administration and practitioners the opportunity to work within the tensions, dilemmas, and contradictions that exist around the theory-practice hyphen.

More importantly, this failure to work the theory-practice hyphen is also partly responsible for the dilemma that characterizes programs of educational administration. Academic faculty tend not to supervise administrative interns because (a) they seldom have recent, if any, experience as administrators and (b) it takes valuable time away from their programmatic research agenda aimed at placing one more brick in the wall of knowledge. These dilemmas fade away once we reconceptualize research as creating action research collaborations among interns, faculty, and critically minded school personnel. Both local and public forms of knowledge can be produced in these collaborations, knowledge that is used immediately within the system, as well as knowledge that academic members of the collaboration can write up for public diffusion through academic and practitioner journals.

Perhaps academics resist collaborative action research because it threatens their expertise, which is built upon years of graduate school socialization into neopositivist forms of quantitative and qualitative research traditions. However, if faculty could just shift their epistemological paradigm a few degrees, they might see that they still have methodological expertise to give to a collaborative enterprise. Unfortunately, action research with practitioners is also viewed as low status in the field. These issues of status would be easier to accept, if the "brick in the wall" programmatic research in our field were of extremely high quality. But as Murphy and his predecessors have copiously documented, that is not the case.

THE DOMINANCE OF TECHNICAL
AND PRACTICAL KNOWLEDGE INTERESTS

While Murphy sprinkles the names of a few critical theorists in the field into this document, the superficial way they appear suggests a "big tent" approach to inclusion of diverse perspectives rather than any understanding of how critical theory might inform the field. While critical theory involves a wide swath of contemporary social theory that in the U.S. context has merged with analyses of race, gender, and sexuality, perhaps the most relevant to this discussion and one that has a long tradition in our field is Jurgens Habermas. Although Habermas's work on communicative action (Foster, 1980) and system and lifeworld (Sergiovanni, 2004) has been more commonly used in our field, I will here draw on his distinctions among the various interests that lie behind the production of knowledge (Habermas, 1971).

As Dan Lortie (1975) long ago documented and others have since reconfirmed, there is a built-in conservatism in schools. Teachers and administrators are immersed in a reified and naturalized world in which common sense is constructed. This commonsense view of school life is, in the language of organizational learning, the administrator's set of theories-in-use. Furthermore, role expectations for legitimation of the status quo are embedded in most organizations and reinforced by their institutional contexts (Anderson, 1990). This problem, which has been noted by many advocates of organizational learning and critical reflection (Robinson, 1993; Tripp, 1994) requires some mechanism that can problematize those taken-for-granted aspects of organizational life. In Habermasian terms, knowledge is not disinterested and a tendency to view knowledge in merely utilitarian terms leads to a distortion of reality that favors keeping things the way they are.

Habermas (1971) pointed out that knowledge and human interests were inseparable. He argued against the claim of the objectivist that valid knowledge could only be generated through methodologies that were empirical-analytical in nature. These research methods attempted to separate what was considered the bias of the researcher from the subject being investigated. However, Habermas insisted that such a separation was an illusion that is ultimately shattered through the process of self-reflection. He maintained that since knowledge was generated through the interest of the mind, "knowledge and interest" are forever linked and cannot be unattached. In refuting the claim of objectivism as the sole pathway to valid knowledge, he presents three distinct "interests" of the researcher in the pursuit of knowledge generation: technical, practical, and emancipatory.

Technical interest focuses upon the human desire to take control over the natural and social realms. Knowledge generated through this orientation historically involved solving technical problems, such as building a fire to keep warm or figuring out how to get from point A to point B. Knowledge generated takes on the form of causal explanations and instrumentation. *Practical* interest refers to an orientation toward gaining understanding through interpretation. Interpretative understanding seeks to generate knowledge that informs and guides practical judgments, the kinds that administrators make every day. The many interpersonal and micropolitical quandaries of school life fall under this knowledge interest.

An *emancipatory* interest orients the researcher toward the release of human potential and the investigation of ideology and power within the organization and society. The ultimate goal of this kind of research is that of the "emancipation of participants from the dictates or compulsions of tradition, precedent, habit, coercion or self-deception" (Carr & Kemmis, 1986). These are thought to be subtle and deeply embedded into the belief structure of the organization and through the process of critical self-reflection can surface and be accessed for examination, ultimately leading to transformation. An understanding of the social changes that have led to the situation described above in which police and metal detectors set the tone of low-income schools (and even many post-Columbine suburban schools) requires a knowledge interest that transcends the technical and the practical. Without this third type of knowledge interest, theories of "distributed leadership," "organizational learning," and "human relations" are understood naively as goals in themselves, rather than potentially as means to other goals, defined outside the school setting. In fact, as I have argued elsewhere, they can become legitimating rituals that serve to make the status quo more palatable (Anderson 1990, 1998).

The distinction among different knowledge interests may help to explain why educational administration programs have not changed dramatically and is useful in explaining why programs tend to unreflectively reproduce current practices. The notion of emancipatory knowledge interests leads to the potential for the "problematization" of current practices as well as one's own unexamined assumptions (Tripp, 1994). In other words, it stresses problem *posing* rather than merely problem *solving*. Although Murphy makes some attempt to set the stage for administrator preparation in changing global economic forces, his analysis—while posturing as even-handed—tends to favor a neoliberal view of the solutions.

RESEARCH IN EDUCATIONAL ADMINISTRATION AS IDEOLOGY

The field of educational administration and the preparation of future administrators are less influenced by research than by ideology. While most researchers today associate "ideology" with scholars who draw on critical theories (critical race theories, feminist theories, neo-Marxist theories, postcolonial theories, and Queer Theory), the ideological influences on the field have for the past 100 years come from business. The lack of a clear understanding of how saturated the field is by business and market ideology means that researchers who fancy themselves untainted by ideology are in fact highly effective conduits of it. A massive body of research documents this influence, such as Callahan's (1962) classic, *The Cult of Efficiency: A Study of the Social Forces That Have Shaped the Administration of Public Schools.* More recently, Thomas Frank (2000) has extended this critique to management literature itself, which he claims provides ideological cover for neoliberal economics.

> Whether Taylorist or humanist, theories of management were sold as a way of defusing class conflict while keeping control of the shop floor firmly in the hands of the owners. As a tool of "nonviolent social control," management theory is, as Barbara Ehrenreich has argued, a close relative of public relations, another profession born at the same time to achieve roughly similar goals. (p. 222)

But who in the field of educational administration knows this history? Where is it taught in administrator-preparation programs? The well-documented links of the human relations movement and union busting are absent from the introductory and organizational theory texts used in our programs (Alex Carey's *Taking the Risk Out of Democracy: Corporate Propaganda Versus Freedom and Liberty* is perhaps the best account). Without a sociohistorical context, organizational and leadership theories become ideologies that support business and market ideology. The history of suburbanization in the postwar years and its class-based and racial effects on housing and schooling are also largely absent from our research and programs. Current forms of market democracy, such as voucher and choice schemes, are a continuation of public policies that stratify our society by race and class, not an interruption of such policies (Margonis & Parker, 1996). Current inequalities in school facilities, school funding, college counseling, and access to AP, gifted, and honors classes, along with an increased military and police presence in low-income schools, are marginal rather than central research agendas in our field. In a section on "reinventing organization and leadership," Murphy reviews literature that critiques bureaucracy and calls for teacher empowerment and shared leadership. Much of this research is rehashed from the business literature and echoes gurus like E. M. Deming and Tom Peters. Behavioral science continues to dominate as new cognitive theories are pressed into service to study "distributed leadership," rather than "democratic leadership." (See Woods, 2004, for a discussion of the distinction.) Although Murphy's characterization of the field is reasonably accurate, we have to ask whose interests are served by such a narrow, mainstream focus.

While good administrators use the principles of organizational learning and distributed leadership (but only if that extends to parents, students, and community organizations), the caring and crucial organizations that such theories can potentially foster should lead to advocacy for low-income children and children of color, not complacency in the face of a neoliberal economic agenda that seeks a weakened, not invigorated, democratic public sphere. The New York City school featured in the vignette in this chapter can be used as a cautionary tale about what happens in public "monopolies." Others might see it as a result of an unrestrained market-based economy that has resulted in a society divided by class and race and a need to create a more invigorated and equitable public sector. The solutions we propose to the problems of both public schooling and public-sector administrator-preparation programs will be largely determined by how we frame the problem.

REFERENCES

Anderson, G. L. (1990). Toward a critical constructivist approach to school administration: Invisibility, legitimation, and the study of non-events. *Educational Administration Quarterly, 26*(1), 38–59.

Anderson, G. L. (1998). Toward authentic participation: Deconstructing the discourse of participatory reforms. *American Educational Research Journal, 35*(4), 571–606.

Anderson, G. L., & Jones, F. (2000). Knowledge generation in educational administration from the inside-out: The promise and perils of site-based, administrator research. *Educational Administration Quarterly, 36*(3), 428–464.

Boyan, N. J. (1981). Follow the leader: Commentary on research in educational administration. *Educational Researcher, 10*(2), 6–13, 21.

Bridges, E. M. (1982). Research on the school administrator: The state of the art, 1967–1980. *Educational Administration Quarterly, 18*(3), 12–33.

Callahan, R. (1962). *Education and the cult of efficiency.* Chicago: The University of Chicago Press.

Carey, A. (1995). *Taking the risk out of democracy: Corporate propaganda versus freedom and liberty.* Urbana: University of Illinois Press.

Carr, W., & Kemmis, S. (1986). *Becoming critical.* London: Falmer Press.

Foster, W. (1980). Administration and the crisis in legitimacy: A review of Habermasian thought. *Harvard Educational Review, 50*(4), 496–505.

Frank, T. (2000). *One market under God: Extreme capitalism, market populism, and the end of economic democracy.* New York: Doubleday.

Habermas, J. (1971). *Knowledge and human interests.* Boston: Beacon Press.

Immegart, G. L. (1990). What is truly missing in advanced preparation in educational administration? *Journal of Educational Administration, 28*(3), 5–13.

Lindblom, C., & Cohen, D. (1979). *Usable knowledge: Social science and social problem solving.* New Haven: Yale University Press.

Lortie, D. (1975). *Schoolteacher.* Chicago: The University of Chicago Press.

Margonis, F., & Parker, L. (1996). School choice in the U.S. urban context: Racism and policies of containment. *Journal of Educational Policy, 11*(6), 717–728.

Pounder, D. G. (2000). A discussion of the task force's collective findings. *Educational Administration Quarterly, 36*(3), 465–473.

Riehl, C., Larson, C. L., Short, P. M., & Reitzug, U. C. (2000). Reconceptualizing research and scholarship in educational administration: Learning to know, knowing to do, and doing to learn. *Educational Administration Quarterly, 36*(3), 391–427.

Robinson, V. (1993). *Problem-based methodology: Research for the improvement of practice.* Oxford, England: Pergamon.

Sergiovanni, T. (2004). *The lifeworld of leadership.* San Francisco: Jossey-Bass.

Tripp, D. (1994). *Critical incidents in teaching: Developing professional judgment.* London: Routledge.

Woods, P. A. (2004). Democratic leadership: drawing distinctions with distributed leadership. *International Journal of Leadership in Education, 7*(1), 3–26.

LEADER PREPARATION RESEARCH PRIORITIES AND REFORM AGENDAS: A RESPONSE TO CHARTING THE CHANGING LANDSCAPE

Diana G. Pounder
University of Utah

Joseph Murphy's book, *Charting the Changing Landscape of the Preparation of School Leaders: An Agenda for Research and Action*, could be characterized in a number of ways. For some, it might read as a full frontal attack on the inadequacies of the behavioral/social science movement in the educational leadership field with a repeated call for "recentering" the profession (and leader preparation) to focus on what Murphy has referred to as "the valued ends of schooling—school improvement, social justice, and democratic community" (Murphy, 1999). For others, this book offers a comprehensive analysis of school administrator preparation during the past century, including (a) the history of leader preparation, analyzed in terms of "periods of ferment" and "change forces"; (b) the concerns of leader preparation programs, including acknowledgement of many significant reform "markers" of the past 20-plus years; (c) the limitations of existing research on leader preparation programs and their effectiveness; and (d) a call for renewed activity and research directed toward improving leadership preparation. Lastly, others will see this work as "connecting the dots" between and among the leadership reform and scholarly endeavors of Murphy and other administrator preparation scholar-leaders during the past two decades, while attempting to get educational leadership academics "on the same page" in a united effort to improve leader-preparation scholarship and action. Perhaps most clearly, this work echoes, reinforces, and strengthens the voices of UCEA leaders and others who have called for and initiated redirected leader preparation research priorities and reform agendas during the past 3 to 5 years.

Let me begin by saying that Murphy's analysis and characterization of leader preparation in our field largely "rings true" for me. That is, his account of historical trends, significant change influences, and general developments in the field of educational administration and school leader preparation are largely similar to my own understandings and observations. Further, his rather comprehensive treatment of the subject helps chronicle the evolution of our field and of leader-preparation program development. However, I believe there are a few omissions that warrant mention to the reader. Thus, I will limit my comments to those issues that I believe may not have received sufficient attention in the book itself.

First, after describing pressures from the environment that call for different understandings of school leadership and leadership preparation, Murphy addresses internal developments that have led to a need to reshape leader preparation. In particular, he addresses (a) the intellectual infrastructure supporting the profession, including research methods, and (b) the methods and procedures to educate school leaders. His analysis leads him to argue that the behavioral/social science movement has failed and that a new "center" for the profession is needed, a center focused on the valued outcomes of schools—school improvement, social justice, and democratic community.

Although I believe that Murphy overstates the shortcomings of the behavioral/social science movement, I nonetheless agree that the educational leadership field or colleges of education in general are not necessarily well served by devotedly mimicking the priorities, trends, norms, or culture of the arts and science disciplines. I have advocated for some time that we may be better served by developing a scholarly and organizational culture that more nearly fits the applied discipline that education is (see Pounder, 2000a). However, rather than reject in entirety the behavioral/social science academic traditions, I would prefer to see us think through which elements do or do not work for us in advancing and improving educational knowledge development, policy, practice, and/or educator preparation.

For example, I would argue that many of the research methods used in the social or behavioral sciences are highly appropriate for use in education and contribute strongly to our field's capacity for knowledge development. Although Murphy very briefly touches upon assessments of the quality of research methods employed in educational leadership studies, he cites only critics of the early 1980s, neglecting to present or discuss the methodological developments of the past 25 years. Specifically, studies employing case study, ethnographic, and other field-based qualitative research designs and methods are now as much or more prevalent as those employing quantitative methods. Further, studies relying upon quantitative methods are no longer limited to survey data with simple descriptive and univariate analyses. Instead, researchers are increasingly using sophisticated designs and analyses intended to capture the complexities and realities of organizational life in schools. As computer technologies have become more available and user friendly, researchers have on their desktop computers with the capacity to analyze large data sets, examining and interpreting complex multivariate relationships among student, teacher, and school data. For example, hierarchical linear modeling (HLM) addresses multilevel effects of students within classrooms within schools within districts within states. Or, causal modeling techniques such as structural equation modeling (SEM) are employed to capture causality and directionality among a complex array of related variables. Additionally, with heightened attention to accountability indicators, more and more studies are using actual school data, often from large national data sets, including student learning indicators and actual school outcome data. Although it is still true that many studies rely largely upon survey data as the primary data source, certainly as many studies today rely upon interview data, with more and more studies using actual field-based school data along with sophisticated and creative analytical techniques to advance knowledge development and address timely educational problems and challenges.

Another omission in Murphy's analysis is the strong emergence and influence of newer research paradigms and methods, such as critical theory, postmodernism, and feminist or race-based epistemologies. Although I am not enough of a scholar of these research approaches to assess their merits or contribution to knowledge development or administrator preparation in educational leadership, there is no denying that they have exercised considerable influence on the research and teaching approaches used by many junior scholars in our field.

I would argue that the methodological and paradigmatic expertise of researchers is becoming increasingly specialized, perhaps creating the unintended consequence of heightened communication and coordination problems among researchers (not to mention school practitioners) addressing similar problems but with quite diverse approaches. I would also argue, as did the first Division A-AERA Task Force on Research and Inquiry, that our field suffers from insufficient "sustained, disciplined, focused empirical inquiry," instead moving from one "hot topic" to the next, leaving only "a shallow pool of research evidence on any given area of focus" (Pounder, 2000b, p. 466). I further concur with the Research and Inquiry Task Force that quality *and* utility are equally important and interdependent research standards in an applied field, such as educational leadership. However, I believe it is no longer accurate to critique our field's methodological approaches for "a pervasive use of survey methods" where "description rather than explanation holds the high ground and univariate analysis predominates" (?).

Another issue that is given only minimal attention in Murphy's analysis and characterization of leader preparation in educational administration is that of changing teaching tools and methods. Murphy criticizes leader-preparation programs as relying largely on lecture and discussion methods and gives only brief attention to the emergence of "problem-based learning" (PBL) and its utility for effective teaching in educational leadership classrooms. There is no mention at all of a fairly long development and implementation history of teaching cases or simulations used in leadership-preparation programs.

Specifically, several decades ago, UCEA colleagues embraced teaching cases as an appropriate and valuable tool for teaching principles of administration and helping students investigate and reflect upon the realities of complex school administrative problems and dilemmas. The development of written cases for use in classroom teaching ultimately led to UCEA's creation and sponsorship of the *Journal of Cases in Educational Leadership* (JCEL) in the mid to late 1990s. The *Journal of Cases* is an electronic journal published three times annually that includes refereed teaching cases and corresponding teaching guidelines developed by scholars in our field for use in leader-preparation classroom teaching. Key promoters and architects of the teaching cases journal included Pat Forsyth and the UCEA Executive Committee, Gary Crow, Mary Driscoll, and Ellen Goldring. The journal was initially housed at the University of Utah, where Gary Crow served as editor; the journal recently moved to Miami University of Ohio, where Michael Dantley serves as editor. UCEA annually awards the Paula Silver Award to the author(s) of the most outstanding JCEL teaching case of the year. This tradition of analyzing teaching cases as a leader-preparation tool can be further evidenced by the number of books devoted largely, if not exclusively, to school administration cases developed for use as teaching tools (see, for example, Cunningham & Cordeiro, 2000; Gorton & Snowden, 1993; Hoy & Tarter, 1995; Kowalski, 2001; Merseth, 1997).

Similarly, the field of educational administration has a rather lengthy history of using administrator simulation exercises in its leader-preparation programs. This history includes a period several decades ago in which the National Association of Secondary School Principals (NASSP) and others (e.g., national foundations) sponsored the development of written and videotaped administrator simulation exercises for use in leader preparation and development, as well as for leader screening/selection. These simulations included NASSP's *Springfield* exercise and *Leader I, II, III* exercises. More recently, in the mid to late 1990s, UCEA, in coordination with the University of Missouri-Columbia and the University of Houston, designed a series of Internet-based school/district reform simulation exercises—one intended to capture the dynamics of rural school district reform (Missouri simulation) and the other intended to capture the dynamics of urban school district reform (Houston simulation).

Lastly, in promoting an agenda for future leader-preparation research and action, there are several issues that I believe warrant more elaboration than offered in this book. First, although Murphy cites the work of several leading scholars who have argued that school administration is largely a moral activity, his discussion and recommendations focus much more on the "intellectual infrastructure supporting the profession" (?) and thus more directly address the intellectual or academic capacity of leaders (i.e., improving leader knowledge and skills) than the moral and dispositional development of leaders. Given the heightened priority of "social justice" in school-leadership preparation, I would argue that a worthy charge for future activity is work specifically focused on how to promote the development of valued moral and dispositional characteristics and behaviors of leaders.

Next, two of the initiatives proposed by Murphy are already under development by the leadership of UCEA. Specifically, a few years ago a national task force headed by Margaret "Terry" Orr and Bob Kottkamp began outlining a research agenda, methods, tools, and strategies for research on the effectiveness of leader-preparation programs, including a strong focus on first-, second-, and third-order program outcomes. That research is now in its initial stage of implementation, with coordinated data collection occurring in 15–20 or more states across the country.

Additionally, UCEA's leadership has already launched preliminary plans to sponsor both a journal and a handbook devoted to scholarship on leader preparation. These initiatives again reflect UCEA's role and commitment to actively promoting and influencing the profession to improve school administrator preparation.

In sum, Murphy's book on "the changing landscape" of school chronicles many of the most important trends and developments in leadership preparation, including many of the past and current contributions of UCEA and its leadership. This book underscores the importance of a coordinated effort to improve administrator preparation and related preparation program research. The book also illustrates and reinforces UCEA's role as a long-standing leader in administrator-preparation reform efforts.

REFERENCES

Cunningham, W. G., & Cordeiro, P. A. (2000). *Educational administration: A problem-based approach.* Boston: Allyn & Bacon.

Gorton, R. A., & Snowden, P. E. (1993). *School leadership and administration: Important concepts, case studies and simulations* (4th ed.). Madison, WI: Brown & Benchmark.

Hoy, W. K., & Tarter, C. J. (1995). *Administrators solving the problems of practice: Decision-making concepts, cases, and consequences.* Boston: Allyn & Bacon.

Kowalski, T. J. (2001). *Case studies on educational administration* (3rd ed.). New York: Longman.

Merseth, K. K. (1997). *Case studies in educational administration.* New York: Longman.

Murphy, J. (1999). *The quest for a center: Notes on the state of the profession of educational leadership.* Columbia, MO: University Council for Educational Administration.

Pounder, D. G. (2000a, Winter). Reflections of and visions for UCEA: 1999 presidential address. *UCEA Review, 41,* 3–5, 12–13.

Pounder, D.G. (2000b). A discussion of the task force's collective findings. *Educational Administration Quarterly, 36*(3), 465–473.

UCEA'S NATIONAL REFORM AGENDA IN ACTION:
AN AFTERWORD

Michelle D. Young
Executive Director, University Council
for Educational Administration

Gary G. Crow
President, University Council for Educational
Administration Professor, University of Utah

Over the past two decades, individuals, associations, consortiums, and commissions have distributed countless reports urging change in educational leadership-preparation programs (Young, Petersen, & Short, 2002). These reports challenged programs and professors to move quickly to implement reform. In response, UCEA, in collaboration with countless higher-education faculty and other committed stakeholders, has become engaged in rethinking and redesigning preparation and research in the field of educational leadership. Joseph Murphy, the author of this UCEA-sponsored book and of many others, has been a constant voice and participant within reform conversations and activities.

This book provides a valuable resource for our field, charting much of the activities and thinking that have brought us to our current location and providing ideas for the field to consider as it works to build a positive and meaningful future. UCEA appreciates the financial support provided by the Wallace Foundation and the leadership provided by the Stanford Finance Project in facilitating Professor Murphy's development of *Preparing School Leaders: Defining a Research and Action Agenda*. UCEA also appreciates the time and effort that professors Diana Pounder and Gary Anderson took to develop thoughtful responses to *Charting the Landscape* as well as that of professor Martha McCarthy, who wrote the foreword for this book. In developing this afterword, we carefully considered the ideas and directions that these influential thinkers offered within the pages of this book, along with the work that UCEA is, has, and plans to do.

In this afterword, we share a draft of UCEA's National Reform Agenda as it is today and as we see it developing over the next few years.

Although we consider higher education to have primary responsibility for making positive, meaningful changes in educational leadership, we propose that it is time for academics and practitioners together to embrace and enact a national reform agenda. We specifically propose three ways that UCEA and its strategic partners can influence the reform of leadership preparation—through ideas, programs, and policy. In all three of these areas, which are described below and contain the current draft of UCEA's National Reform Agenda, the valuable recommendations expressed by the contributors to this book can be realized, and as you will find, several are already in place.

INFLUENCING IDEAS

In the current context of critiques of educational leadership preparation, scholars have tended to react to these criticisms rather than to proactively influence ideas. As Anderson's response in this book clearly emphasizes, we need to question assumptions, such as the appropriateness of market solutions to educational challenges, and to critically examine leadership preparation in the context of its purposes, its current realities, and its future possibilities.

One current attempt to engage scholars in influencing ideas about leadership preparation is the Research Task Force on Leader Preparation, jointly sponsored by UCEA, the American Educational Research Association (AERA)-Division A, AERA's Teaching in Educational Administration Special Interest Group (TEA Sig), and the National Council for Professors of Educational Administration (NCPEA). This task force focuses on many of the structural elements identified by Murphy and elaborated on by Pounder and Anderson, including the context of leadership preparation, both university-based and alternative-preparation models, theories, recruitment and selection, providers, curriculum and pedagogy, delivery, assessment, professional learning, and global perspectives. The scholars involved in the 10 domains of the task force are currently exploring and describing the leadership preparation landscape, identifying research gaps and commissioning papers and studies to fill these gaps.

A closely related project, also sponsored by UCEA in collaboration with scholars from AERA and NCPEA, is the *Handbook of Research on*

Leadership Education. This venture, which was called for by Murphy in this book and elsewhere (e.g., Murphy & Vriesenga, 2004), will bring together junior and senior colleagues to collect and distribute conceptual and empirical work on the various elements of leadership preparation. The task force and the handbook are aimed at influencing the conversations and debates that are crucial in not only expanding our knowledge but also enriching our practice. In a similar vein, UCEA is collaborating with the British Educational Leadership, Management and Administration Society (BELMAS) and the Commonwealth Council for Educational Administration and Management (CCEAM) in the development of the *International Handbook of Research on Leadership Education*. The international handbook will provide valuable reviews of leadership preparation and development practice and research in a large number of countries around the globe, as well as comparative reviews across countries.

UCEA has also developed a new electronic journal, *The Journal of Research on Leadership Education* (JRLE), to influence ideas around leadership preparation. The journal, edited by Edith Rusch and her colleagues at the University of Nevada, Las Vegas, will be a peer-refereed journal, publishing empirical and conceptual pieces on leadership-preparation program components. It is designed to encourage an open and provocative exchange of ideas among professors, students, and practitioners in education and other social sciences in an interdisciplinary environment. Such a vehicle should create a timely and lively environment for critical conversations around the complex issues of leadership preparation reform.

Of course, educational leadership programs are not limited to the preparation of leaders and the conduct of research on leadership issues. UCEA leadership programs are also engaged in the development of future leadership scholars. For many years, UCEA has provided mentorship, networking, and research opportunities for faculty and doctoral students. The David L. Clark Graduates Student Research Seminar, the UCEA Graduate Student Symposia, and more recently, UCEA's development of the Barbara L. Jackson Scholars network are good examples of such activities. UCEA is searching for ways to build on these and other past successes to provide even more meaningful professional development experiences to doctoral students and faculty alike.

In addition to influencing ideas through task forces, handbooks, journals, and conversations that are focused primarily toward an academic audience, UCEA is also committed to opening up these critical conversations to include practitioners. Submitting articles and papers to practitioner magazines, professional conferences, and major forums that include practitioners, policymakers, and professors will help to broaden the discussion of ideas, take advantage of multiple perspectives, and create more open dialogue around the issues of leadership-preparation reform.

INFLUENCING PROGRAMS

Frequently, professors are criticized for ignoring the call for preparation program reforms and for being complacent with the existence of poor programs. A critical and open acknowledgment that leadership-preparation programs can and should improve is vital to our credibility to contribute to the national reform agenda. One way that UCEA influences leadership-preparation programs is to provide standards and mechanisms to aid programs in evaluating and improving themselves.

UCEA has provided a set of rigorous program standards for its member institutions for more than 50 years, and as the field developed, UCEA frequently evaluated and redeveloped its standards to ensure they continued to reflect excellence in the preparation of leaders for and researchers of field of education. UCEA also participated in the development of standards for school and district leadership practice, such as the Interstate School Leadership Licensure Consortium (ISLLC). Most recently, UCEA has undertaken the task of identifying program and content standards and expectations for the development of educational leaders at the master's and doctorate levels (M.Ed. and Ed.D.) and the preparation of educational researchers at the doctorate level (PhD).

UCEA is also in the midst of revising its program review process. The initial review involves the development of a program portfolio aligned to UCEA program standards, a site visit, and reviews of these materials by the UCEA Executive Committee and Plenum. The continuing review (formerly called the UCEA sabbatical review) has followed this same pattern in the past, but UCEA now has plans to align its continuing review with the review provided by national, state, and regional accrediting bodies.

Although there are valid debates regarding the use of accreditation bodies, particularly national accreditation bodies, the work of these organizations has been significant for identifying areas for reform and developing standards for leadership-preparation programs. We believe it is vital that UCEA, individual leadership programs, and other professional organizations participate in and contribute to the work of accrediting bodies, such as NCATE and TEAC, in order to influence valid, rigorous, and purposeful assessments and reforms of leadership-preparation programs.

UCEA leadership has also considered the costs and benefits of deeper involvement in the accreditation process. A recent proposal suggested that UCEA, by itself or in conjunction with other groups, such as NCPEA, should develop and offer an accreditation specifically for university leadership-preparation programs. Using models, such as the American Psychological Association or a Critical Friends Approach, UCEA could not only provide a valuable service to preparation programs but also influence program quality.

Similarly, UCEA leadership has considered how UCEA, by itself or in conjunction with other professional organizations, might provide leadership programs with instruments to conduct valid and rigorous self-studies as well as guidance for program improvement. Evaluation instruments would be used to facilitate self-studies aimed at identifying program strengths and areas for program improvement. The instruments would be based both on standards and the latest research on effective leadership programs. In addition to providing such instruments, however, it has been suggested that UCEA act as a clearinghouse or data repository center. In this capacity, UCEA would collect information from program evaluation and improvement efforts that could be used both by programs and for responding to critiques and calls for reform in the field. At the present time, UCEA is working with the members of the Teaching in Educational Administration special-interest group on the development of evaluation instruments.

UCEA has, for many years, provided the field with high-quality instructional materials. UCEA has developed or sponsored the development of simulations, case studies, problem-based learning units, and teaching modules. UCEA will continue to provide such materials and has plans for (1) increased technological enhancement and integration, (2) stronger alignment with UCEA and other sets of leadership standards, (3) cooperative materials development projects with strategic partners (e.g., AERA, Vermont Institute for Individuals with Disabilities and Students Placed at Risk, and (4) wider distribution.

INFLUENCING POLICY

A national reform agenda must also involve influencing policies and policymakers in the substantive and complex nature of leadership-preparation
reform. Focusing only on our scholarly conversations and programs without recognizing that reform must occur at various levels will limit our credibility and influence. In its efforts to positively influence local, state, and national educational policy, UCEA intends to leverage its work with the
National Commission for the Advancement of Educational Leadership
Preparation (NCAELP), the National Policy Board for Educational Administration (NPBEA), UCEA Program Centers, and its membership network.

UCEA plans to continue the work of the National Commission for the
Advancement of Educational Leadership Preparation (NCAELP) by holding a national meeting in the near future to polish and operationalize a final version of this National Reform Agenda. Part of operationalizing the
agenda will be the development of a series of white papers articulating
and outlining specific areas of the agenda, including, as Murphy suggested in his recommendation section, a paper that sets the agenda for research on preparation. The national meeting will be followed by regional
forums to provide information to stakeholders, including state policymakers who are exerting a greater amount of influence on such leadership-
preparation issues as certification and licensure, program approvals, and
alternative delivery systems. UCEA hopes to establish NCAELP regional
forums in which legislators, offices of education officials, governors, professors, university officials, and district partners are invited to share concerns and ideas for enriching leadership preparation.

Influencing policy is seldom successful if done in a vacuum. UCEA and
other professional organizations must build alliances in and across the
field. Alliances with members of the National Policy Board, especially
NCPEA, directors of UCEA Program Centers, political activist groups,
constituents, and others are necessary to present a united and strong front
to influence policymakers on enriching leadership preparation. These alliances help to establish credibility for UCEA and others as informed and
committed partners in building strong and effective leadership preparation
programs.

It is also crucial that UCEA and other organizations continue to be
proactive in responding to critiques of educational leadership preparation,

such as those contained within the recent reports from the American Enterprise Institute and the Education Schools Project. Responses must continue to be constructive rather than defensive and must use the research
that is developing on what constitutes effective programs and the current
landscape of leadership preparation.

CONCLUSION

As the reform agenda demonstrates, UCEA actively initiates and leads educational reform efforts through its high-quality research and preparation
programs. Indeed, UCEA has a long history of working collaboratively to
positively advance the preparation and practice of educational leaders for
the benefit of schools and children. As a community, we support this important goal by (1) promoting, sponsoring, and disseminating research on
the essential problems of schooling, leadership practice, and leadership
preparation; (2) improving the preparation and professional development
of educational leaders and professors; and (3) positively influencing
local, state, and national educational policies. We hope that all of those
reading this book will join with us as we work for positive change within
educational-leadership programs and the field at large.

REFERENCES

Murphy, J., & Vriesenga, M. (2004). *Research on preparation programs in edu-
cational administration: An analysis.* Columbia, MO: University Council for
Educational Administration.
Young, M. D., Petersen, G. J., & Short, P. M. (2002). The complexity of substan-
tive reform: A call for interdependence among key stakeholders. *Educational
Administration Quarterly, 38* (2), 137–175.

References

‡

Achilles, C. M. (1984). Forecast: Stormy weather ahead in educational administration. *Issues in Education 2*(2), 127–135.

American Association of Colleges for Teacher Education. (1988). *School leadership preparation: A preface for action.* Washington, DC: Author.

American Association of School Administrators. (1960). *Professional administrators for America's schools* (38th AASA Yearbook).

Anderson, G. L. (1990). Toward a critical constructionist approach to school administration: Invisibility, legitimization, and the study of non-events. *Educational Administration Quarterly 26*(1), 38–59.

Anderson, R. C., Hiebert, E. H., Scott, J. A., & Wilkinson, I. A. G. (1985). *Becoming a nation of readers: The Report of the Commission on Reading.* Washington, D.C.: The National Institute of Education, U.S. Department of Education.

Anderson, W. A., & Lonsdale, R. C. (1957). Learning administrative behavior. In R. F. Campbell & R. T. Gregg (Eds.), *Administrative behavior in education* (pp. 426–463). New York: Harper.

Bailey, R. W. (1987). Uses and misuses of privatization. In S. H. Hanke (Ed.), *Proceedings of the Academy of Political Science: Vol. 36, No. 3. Prospects for privatization* (pp. 138–152). Montpelier, VT: Capital City Press.

Banathy, B. H. (1988). An outside-in approach to design inquiry in education. In *The redesign of education: Vol. 1. A collection of papers concerned with comprehensive educational reform* (pp. 51–71). San Francisco: Far West Laboratory for Educational Research and Development.

Barber, B. R. (1984). *Strong democracy: Participatory politics for a new age.* Berkeley: University of California Press.

Barnett, B., Basom, M., Yerkes, D. & Norris, C. (2000). Cohorts in educational leadership programs: Benefits, difficulties and the potential for developing school leaders. *Educational Administration Quarterly 36*(2), 255–282.

Barth, R. S. (1986). On sheep and goats and school reform. *Phi Delta Kappan 68*(4), 293–296.

Barth, R. S. (1988). School: A community of leaders. In A. Lieberman (Ed.), *Building a professional culture in schools* (pp. 129–147). New York: Teachers College Press.

Barth, R. S. (2001). Teacher leader. *Phi Delta Kappan 82*(6), 443–449.

Bates, R. J. (1984). Toward a critical practice of educational administration. In T. J. Sergiovanni & J. E. Corbally (Eds.), *Leadership and organizational culture: New perspectives on administrative theory and practice* (pp. 360–274). Urbana: University of Illinois Press.

Bauman, P. C. (1996). Governing education in an antigovernment environment. *Journal of School Leadership 6*(6), 625–643.

Beare, H. (1989, September). *Educational Administration in the 1990s.* Paper presented at the national conference of the Australian Council for Educational Administration, Armidale, New South Wales, Australia.

Beck, L. G. (1994). *Reclaiming educational administration as a caring profession.* New York: Teachers College Press.

Beck, L. G., & Foster, W. (1999). Administration and community: Considering challenges, exploring possibilities. In J. Murphy & K. S. Louis (Eds.). *Handbook of research on educational administration* (pp. 337–358). San Francisco: Jossey-Bass.

Beck, L. G., & Murphy, J. (1993). *Understanding the principalship: A metaphorical analysis, 1920s–1990s.* New York: Teachers College Press.

Beck, L. G., & Murphy, J. (1994). *Ethics in educational leadership programs: An expanding role.* Thousand Oaks, CA: Corwin.

Beck, L. G., Murphy, J., & Associates. (1997a). *Ethics in educational leadership preparation programs: Emerging models.* Newbury Park, CA: Corwin Press.

Beck, L. G., Murphy, J., & Associates. (1997b). *Ethics in educational leadership preparation programs: An expanding role.* Newbury Park, CA: Corwin Press.

Beers, D., & Ellig, J. (1994). An economic view of the effectiveness of public and private schools. In S. Hakim, P. Seidenstat & G. W. Bowman (Eds.), *Privatizing education and educational choice: Concepts, plans, and experiences* (pp. 19–38). Westport, CT: Praeger.

Bishop, H. L., Tinley, A., & Berman, B. T. (1997). A contemporary leadership model to promote teacher leadership. *Action in Teacher Education 19*(3), 77–81.

Björk, L. G., & Ginsberg, R. (1995). Principles of reform and reforming principal training: A theoretical perspective. *Educational Administration Quarterly 31*(1), 11–37.

Bolin, F. S. (1989). Empowering leadership. *Teachers College Record 91*(1), 81–96.

Boyan, N. J. (1963). Common and specialized learnings for administrators and supervisors: Some problems and issues. In D. J. Leu & H. C. Rudman (Eds.), *Preparation programs for school administrators: Common and specialized learnings* (pp. 1–23). East Lansing: Michigan State University.

Boyan, N. J. (1981). Follow the leader: Commentary on research in educational administration. *Educational Research 10*(2), 6–13, 21.

Boyan, N. J. (1988a). Describing and explaining administrator behavior. In N. J. Boyan (Ed.), *Handbook of research on educational* administration. New York: Longman.

Boyan, N. J. (Ed.). (1988b). *Handbook of research on educational administration.* New York: Longman.

Brent, B. O. (1998). Should graduate training in educational administration be required for principal certification? Existing evidence suggests the answer is no. *Teaching in Educational Administration 5*(2), 1, 3–4, 7–10.

Bridges, E. M. (1977). The nature of leadership. In L. L. Cunningham, W. G. Hack, & R. O. Nystrand (Eds.), *Educational administration: The developing decades* (pp. 202–230). Berkeley, CA: McCutchan.

Bridges, E. M. (1982). Research on the school administrator: The state of the art, 1967–1980. *Educational Administration Quarterly 18*(3), 12–33.

Burke, C. (1992). Devolution of responsibility to Queensland schools: Clarifying the rhetoric critiquing the reality. *Journal of Educational Administration 30*(4), 33–52.

Button, H. W. (1966). Doctrines of administration: A brief history. *Educational Administration Quarterly 2*(3), 216–224.

Callahan, R. E. (1962). *Education and the cult of efficiency.* Chicago: University of Chicago Press.

Callahan, R. E., & Button, H. W. (1964). Historical change of the role of the man in the organization: 1865–1950. In D. E. Griffiths (Ed.), *Vol. 63, Behavioral science and educational administration* (pp. 73–92). Chicago: University of Chicago Press.

Campbell, R. F. (1979). A critique of the *Educational Administration Quarterly. Educational Administration Quarterly 15*(3), 1–19.

Campbell, R. F. (1981). The professorship in educational administration: A personal view. *Educational Administration Quarterly 71*(1), 1–24.

Campbell, R. F., Fleming, T., Newell, L. J., & Bennion, J. W. (1987). *A history of thought and practice in educational administration.* New York: Teachers College Press.

Campbell, R. F., & Newell, L. J. (1973). *A study of professors of educational administration: Problems and prospects of an applied academic field.* Columbus, OH: University Council for Educational Administration.

Chall, J. S., Jacobs, V. A., & Baldwin, L. E. (1990). *The reading crisis: Why poor children fall behind.* Cambridge, MA: Harvard University Press.

Chase, F. S. (1960). The administrator as implementor of the goals of education for our time. In R. F. Campbell & J. M. Lipham (Eds.), *Administrative theory as a guide to action* (pp. 191–201). Chicago: University of Chicago, Midwest Administration Center.

Chenoweth, T. G., & Everhart, R. B. (2002). *Navigating comprehensive school change: A guide for the perplexed.* Larchmont, NY: Eye on Education.

Childs-Bowen, D., Moller, G., & Scrivner, J. (2000, May). Principals: Leaders of leaders. *NASSP Bulletin 84*(616), 27–34.

Cibulka, J. G. (1999). Ideological lenses for interpreting political and economic changes affecting schooling. In J. Murphy & K. S. Louis (Eds.), *Handbook of research on educational administration* (2nd ed., pp. 163–182). San Francisco: Jossey-Bass.

Clark, D. L. (1987, August). *Thinking about leaders and followers: Restructuring the roles of principals and teachers.* Paper presented at the conference on Restructuring Schooling for Quality Education, Trinity University, San Antonio, TX.

Clark, D. L. (1988, June). *Charge to the study group of the National Policy Board for Educational Administration.* Unpublished manuscript.

Clark, D. L., & Meloy, J. M. (1989). Renouncing bureaucracy: A democratic structure for leadership in schools. In T. J. Sergiovanni & J. A. Moore (Eds.), *Schooling for tomorrow: Directing reform to issues that count* (pp. 272–294). Boston: Allyn & Bacon.

Cohen, D. K. (1988, September). *Teaching practice: Plus ça change . . .* (Issue Paper 88-3). East Lansing: Michigan State University, National Center for Research on Teacher Education.

Conley, S. C. (1989, March). *Who's on first? School reform, teacher participation, and the decision-making process.* Paper presented at the annual meeting of the American Research Association, San Francisco.

Conley, D. T. (1997). *Roadmap to restructuring: Charting the course of change in American education.* Eugene, OR: ERIC Clearinghouse on Educational Management.

Consortium on Productivity in the Schools. (1995). *Using what we have to get the schools we need.* New York: Columbia University, Teachers College, The Institute on Education and the Economy.

Cooley, W. W., & Leinhardt, G. (1980). The instructional dimensions study. *Educational Evaluation and Policy Analysis 2*(1), 7–25.

Cooper, B. S., & Boyd, W. L. (1987). The evolution of training for school administrators. In J. Murphy & P. Hallinger (Eds.), *Approaches to administrative training* (pp. 3–27). Albany, NY: SUNY Press.

Cooper, B. S., & Muth, R. (1994). Internal and external barriers to change in departments of educational administration. In T. A. Mulkeen, N. H. Cambron-McCabe, & B. J. Anderson (Eds.), *Democratic leadership: The changing context of administrative preparation* (pp. 61–81). Norwood, NJ: Ablex.

Copland, M. A. (2003). Building the capacity to lead: Promoting and sustaining change in an inquiry-based model of school reform. In J. Murphy & A. Datnow (Eds.), *Leadership for school reform: Lessons from comprehensive school reform designs* (pp. 159–183). Thousand Oaks, CA: Corwin Press.

Corcoran, T. B. (1989). Restructuring education: A new vision at Hope Essential High School. In J. M. Rossow & R. Zager (Eds.), *Allies in educational reform* (pp. 243–274). San Francisco: Jossey-Bass.

Cotton, K. & Savard, W. G. (1980, December). *Parent participation.* Paper prepared for Alaska Department of Education, Office of Planning and Research, Audit and Evaluation Program, Northwest Education Laboratory, Portland, OR.

Creighton, T. (1997, March). *Teachers as leaders: Is the principal really needed?* Paper presented at the annual conference on Creating Quality Schools, Oklahoma City. (ERIC Documentation Reproductive Service No. ED411117)

Creighton, T. (2002). Standards for educational administration preparation programs: Okay, but don't we have the cart before the horse? *Journal of School Leadership 12*(5), 526–551.

Cronin, T. E. (1989). *Direct democracy: The politics of initiative, referendum, and recall.* Cambridge, MA: Harvard University Press.

Crow, G. M., Hausman, C. S., & Scribner, J. P. (2002). Reshaping the role of the school principal. In J. Murphy (Ed.), *The educational leadership challenge: Redefining leadership for the 21st century* (pp. 189–210). Chicago: University of Chicago Press.

Crowson, R. L., & McPherson, R. B. (1987). The legacy of the theory movement: Learning from the new tradition. In J. Murphy & P. Hallinger (Eds.), *Approaches to administrative training in education* (pp. 45–64). Albany, NY: SUNY Press.

Crowther, F., Kaagan, S. S., Ferguson, M., & Hann, L. (2002). *Developing teacher leaders: How teacher leadership enhances school success.* Thousand Oaks, CA: Corwin Press.

Cuban, L. (1989). The "at-risk" label and the problem of school reform. *Phi Delta Kappan 70*(10), 780–84, 799.

Culbertson, J. A. (1963). Common and specialized content in the preparation of administrators. In D. J. Leu & H. C. Rudman (Eds.), *Preparation programs for administrators: Common and specialized learnings* (pp. 34–60). East Lansing: Michigan State University.

Culbertson, J. A. (1964). The preparation of administrators. In D. E. Griffiths (Ed.), *Behavioral science in educational administration* (63rd NSSE yearbook, Part II, pp. 303–330). Chicago: University of Chicago Press.

Culbertson, J. A. (1965). Trends and issues in the development of a science of administration. In *Perspectives on Educational Administration and the Behavioral Sciences* (pp. 3–32). Eugene, OR: Center for the Advanced Study of Educational Administration.

Culbertson, J. A. (1988). A century's quest for a knowledge base. In N. J. Boyan (Ed.), *Handbook of research on educational administration* (pp. 3–26). New York: Longman.

Culbertson, J. A., & Farquhar, R. H. (1971, January). Preparing educational leaders: Content in administration preparation. *UCEA Review 12*(3), 8–11.

Culbertson, T. (1995). *Building bridges: UCEA's first two decades.* University Park, PA: University Council for Educational Administration.

Dahrendorf, R. (1995, Summer). A precarious balance: Economic opportunity, civil society and political liberty. *The Responsive Community,* 13–19.

Daresh, J. C. (1987). The practicum in preparing educational administrators: A status report. Paper presented at the Eastern Educational Research Association Meeting, Boston.

David, J. (1989). *Restructuring in progress: Lessons from pioneering districts.* Washington, DC: National Governors' Association.

Denham, C., & Leiberman, A. (Eds.) (1980). *Time to learn.* Washington, DC: National Institute of Education.

Donahue, J. D. (1989). *The privatization decision: Public ends, private means.* New York: Basic Books.

Donaldson, G. A. (2001). *Cultivating leadership in schools: Connecting people, purpose, and practice.* New York: Teachers College Press.

Donmoyer, R. (1999). The continuing quest for a knowledge base: 1976–1998. In J. Murphy & K. S. Louis (Eds.), *Handbook of research on educational administration* (2nd ed., pp. 25–43). San Francisco: Jossey-Bass.

Donmoyer, R., Imber, M., & Scheurich, J. J. (Eds.) (1995). *The knowledge base in educational administration: Multiple perspectives.* Albany, NY: State University of New York Press.

Elmore, R. F. (1989, March). *Models of restructured schools.* Paper presented at the annual meeting of the American Educational Research Association, San Francisco.

Elmore, R. F. (1990, September). *Reinventing school leadership* (pp. 62–65) [Working memo prepared for the Reinventing School Leadership Conference]. Cambridge, MA: National Center for Educational Leadership.

Elmore, R. F. (1993). School decentralization: Who gains? Who loses? In J. Hannaway & M. Carnoy (Eds.), *Decentralization and school improvement* (pp. 33–54). San Francisco: Jossey-Bass.

Elmore, R. F. (1996, March). *Staff development and instructional improvement: Community District 2, New York City.* Paper presented for the National Commission on Teaching and America's Future (Draft).

Elmore, R. F. (2000). *Building a new structure for school leadership.* Washington, DC: Albert Shanker Institute.

Elmore, R. F. (2003). Accountability and capacity. In M. Carnoy, R. Elmore, & L. S. Siskin (Eds.), *High schools and the new accountability* (pp. 195–209). New York: Routledge.

Elmore, R. F., Peterson, P. L., & McCarthy, S. J. (1996). *Restructuring in the classroom: Teaching, learning, and school organization.* San Francisco: Jossey-Bass.

Elshtain, J. B. (1995). *Democracy on trial.* New York: Basic Books.

English, F. W. (1997). The cupboard is bare: The postmodern critique of educational administration. *Journal of School Leadership* 7(1), 4–26.

Erickson, D. A. (1967). The school administrator. *Review of Educational Research 37*(4), 417–432.

Erickson, D. A. (1977). An overdue paradigm shift in educational administration, or how can we get that idiot off the freeway. In L. L. Cunningham, W. G. Hack, & R. O. Nystrand (Eds.), *Educational administration: The developing decades* (pp. 114–143). Berkeley, CA: McCutchan.

Erickson, D. A. (1979). Research on educational administration: The state-of-the-art. *Educational Researcher 8*, 9–14.

Erlandson, D. A., & Witters-Churchill, L. (1988, March). *Design of the Texas NASSP study.* Paper presented at the annual convention of the National Association of Secondary School Principals.

Evans, R. (1991, April). *Ministrative insight: Educational administration as a pedagogic practice.* Paper presented at the annual meeting of the American Educational Research Association, Chicago.

Evans, R. (1998). Do intentions matter? Questioning the text of a high school principal. *Journal of Educational Administration and Foundations 13*(1), 30–51.

Farquhar, R. H. (1977). Preparatory program in educational administration. In L. L. Cunningham, W. G. Hack, & R. O. Nystrand (Eds.), *Educational administration: The developing decades* (pp. 329–357). Berkeley, CA: McCutchan.

Farquhar, R. H. (1981). Preparing educational administrators for ethical practice. *The Alberta Journal of Educational Research, 27*(2), 192–204.

Fay, C. (1992a, April). *The case for teacher leadership: Toward definition and development.* Paper presented at the annual meeting of the American Educational Research Association, San Francisco.

Fay, C. (1992b). Empowerment through leadership: In the teachers' voice. In C. Livingston (Ed.), *Teachers as leaders: Evolving roles* (pp. 57–90). Washington, DC: National Education Association.

Ferguson, R. F., & Ladd, H. F. (1996). How and why does money matter: An analysis in Alabama schools. In G. Burtless (Ed.), *Does money matter: The effect of school resources on student achievement and adult success.* Washington, D.C.: Brookings.

Firestone, W. A. (1996). Leadership roles or functions. In K. Leithwood, J. Chapman, D. Corson, P. Hallinger, & A. Hart (Eds.), *International handbook of educational leadership and administration* (pp. 395–418). Dordrecht: Kluwer.

Firestone, W. A., & Riehl, C. (2003). *Prospectus for the volume of the task force on research and inquiry in educational administration.*

Fisher, C., & Adler, M. A. (1999). *Early reading programs in high-poverty schools: Emerald Elementary beats the odds.* Ann Arbor: University of Michigan, Center for the Improvement of Early Reading Achievement.

Forster, E. M. (1997). Teacher leadership: Professional right and responsibility. *Action in Teacher Education 19*(3), 82–94.

Forsyth, P. (1999). A brief history of scholarship on educational administration. In J. Murphy & P. Forsyth (Eds.), *Educational administration: A decade of reform* (pp. 71–92). Newbury Park, CA: Corwin Press.

Forsyth, P. B., & Murphy, J. (1999). A decade of changes: Analyses and comments. In J. Murphy & P. B. Forsyth (Eds.), *Educational administration: A decade of reform* (pp. 253–272). Thousand Oaks, CA: Corwin Press.

Forsyth, P. B., & Willower, D. J. (1999). A brief history of scholarship on educational administration. In J. Murphy & K. S. Louis (Eds.), *Handbook of research on educational administration* (2nd ed., pp. 1–23). San Francisco: Jossey-Bass.

Foster, W. (1986). *Paradigms and promises: New approaches to educational administration.* Buffalo, NY: Prometheus.

Foster, W. (1988). Educational administration: A critical appraisal. In D. E. Griffiths, R. T. Stout, & R. B. Forsyth (Eds.), *Leaders for America's schools* (pp. 68–81). Berkeley, CA: McCutchan.

Frost, D., & Durant, J. (2003). Teacher leadership: Rationale, strategy, and impact. *School Leadership & Management 23*(2), 173–186.

Frymier, J. (1987). Bureaucracy and the neutering of teachers. *Phi Delta Kappan 69*(1), 9–14.

Fullan, M. (2004). *The moral imperative of school leadership.* Thousand Oaks, CA: Corwin Press.

Fusarelli, L. D., & Scribner, J. D. (1993, October). *Site-based management and critical democratic pluralism: An analysis of promises, problems, and possibilities.* Paper presented at the annual conference of the University Council for Educational Administration, Houston, TX.

Gerritz, W., Koppich, J., & Guthrie, J. (1984). *Preparing California school leaders: An analysis of supply, demand, and training.* Berkeley: University of California, Policy Analysis for California Education.

Getzels, J. W. (1977). Educational administration twenty years later, 1954–1974. In L. L. Cunningham, W. G. Hack, & R. O. Nystrand (eds.), Educational administration: The developing decades (pp. 3–24). Berkeley, CA: McCutchan.

Giroux, H. A. (1988). *Teachers as intellectuals: Toward a critical pedagogy of learning.* Granby, MA: Bergin & Garvey.

Glasman, N., Cibulka, J., & Ashby, D. (2002). Program self-evaluation for continuous improvement. *Educational Administration Quarterly 38*(2), 257–288.

Glass, T. E. (1986). *An analysis of texts on school administration 1820–1985.* Danville, IL: Interstate.

Glickman, C. D. (1990). Pushing school reform to a new edge: The seven ironies of school empowerment. *Phi Delta Kappan 71*(1), 68–75.

Goldhammer, K. (1983). Evolution in the profession. *Educational Administration Quarterly 19*(3), 249–272.

Goodlad, J. I. (1984). *A place called school: Prospects for the future.* New York: McGraw-Hill.

Gottfried, P. (1993). *The conservative movement* (Rev. ed.). New York: Twayne.

Grace, A. G. (1946). The professional preparation of school personnel. In N. B. Henry (Ed.), *Changing conceptions in educational administration* (45th NSSE yearbook, Part II, pp. 176–182). Chicago: University of Chicago Press.

Graff, O. B., & Street, C. M. (1957). Developing a value framework for educational administration. In R. F. Campbell & R. T. Gregg (Eds.), *Administrative Behavior in Education* (pp. 120–152). New York: Harper.

Greenfield, T. B. (1975). Theory about organization: A new perspective and its implications for schools. In M. G. Hughes (Ed.), *Administering education: International challenge* (pp. 71–99). London: Athlone.

Greenfield, T. B. (1988). The decline and fall of science in educational administration. In D. E. Griffiths, R. T. Stout, & P. B. Forsyth (Eds.), *Leaders for America's schools* (pp. 131–159). Berkeley, CA: McCutchan.

Greenfield, W. (1995). Toward a theory of school administration: The centrality of leadership. *Educational Administration Quarterly 31*(1), 61–85.

Gregg, R. T. (1960). Administration. In C. W. Harris (Ed.), *Encyclopedia of educational research* (3rd ed., pp. 19–24). New York: Macmillan.

Gregg, R. T. (1969). Preparation of administrators. In R. L. Ebel (Ed.), *Encyclopedia of educational research* (4th ed., pp. 993–1004). London: Macmillan.

Griffiths, D. E. (1959). *Administrative theory.* New York: Appleton-Century-Crofts.

Griffiths, D. E. (1965). Research and theory in educational administration. In *Perspectives on educational administration and the behavioral sciences* (pp. 25–48). Eugene: University of Oregon, Center for the Advanced Study of Educational Administration.

Griffiths, D. E. (1988a). *Educational administration: Reform PDQ or RIP* (Occasional paper, no. 8312). Tempe, AZ: University Council for Educational Administration.

Griffiths, D. E. (1988b). Administrative theory. In N. J. Boyan (Ed.), *Handbook of research on educational administration* (pp. 27–51). New York: Longman.

Griffiths, D. E. (1997). The case for theoretical pluralism. *Educational Management & Administration 25*(4), 371–380.

Griffiths, D. E., Stout, R. T., & Forsyth, P. B. (1988a). *Leaders for America's schools: The report and papers of the National Commission on Excellence in Educational Administration.* Berkeley, CA: McCutchan.

Griffiths, D. E., Stout, R. T., & Forsyth, P. B. (1988b). The preparation of educational administrators. In D. E. Griffiths, R. T. Stout, & P. B. Forsyth (Eds.), *Leaders for America's schools: The report and papers of the National Commission on Excellence in Educational Administration.* Berkeley, CA: McCutchan.

Grogan, M., & Andrews, R. (2003). Defining preparation and professional development for the future. *Educational Administration Quarterly 38*(2), 233–256.

Guba, E. G. (1960). Research in internal administration—What do we know? In R. F. Campbell & J. M. Lipham (Eds.), *Administrative theory as a guide to action* (pp. 113–141). Chicago: University of Chicago, Midwest Administrative Center.

Guthrie, J. W. (1986). School-based management: The next needed educational reform. *Phi Delta Kappan 68*(4), 305–309.

Guthrie, J. W. (1997, October). The paradox of educational power: How modern reform proposals miss the point. *Education Week 17*(7), 34.

Hakim, S., Seidenstat, P., & Bowman, G. W. (1994). Introduction. In Hakim, S., Seidenstat, P., & Bowman, G. W. (eds.), Privatizing education and educational choice: Concepts, plans, and experiences (pp. 1–15). Westport, CT: Praeger.

Hakim, S., Seidenstat, P., & Bowman, G. W. (1994). *Privatizing education and educational choice: Concepts, plans, and experiences.* Westport, CT: Praeger.

Hall, R. M., & McIntyre, K. E. (1957). The student personnel program. In R. F. Campbell & R. T. Gregg (eds.), Administrative behavior in education (pp. 393–425). New York: Harper.

Haller, E. J., Brent, B. O., & McNamara, J. H. (1997). Does graduate training in educational administration improve America's schools? *Phi Delta Kappan 79*(3), 222–227.

Hallinger, P. (1981). *Review of the school effectiveness research.* Paper prepared for the Carnegie Foundation.

Hallinger, P., Leithwood, K., & Murphy, J. (Eds.) (1993). *A cognitive perspective on educational administration.* New York: Teachers College Press.

Hallinger, P., & Murphy, J. (1991, March). Developing leaders for tomorrow's schools. *Phi Delta Kappan 72*(7), 514–520.

Halpin, A. W. (1957). A paradigm for research on administrative behavior. In R. F. Campbell & R. T. Gregg (eds.), *Administrative behavior in education* (pp. 155–199). New York: Harper.

Halpin, A. W. (1960). Ways of knowing. In R. F. Campbell & J. M. Lipham (Eds.), *Administrative theory as a guide to action* (pp. 3–20). Chicago: University of Chicago, Midwest Administrative Center.

Hannaway, J., & Crowson, R. (Eds.) (1989). *The politics of reforming school administration.* New York: Falmer.

Hanson, E. M. (1991). *School-based management and educational reform: Cases in the USA and Spain.* (ERIC Document Reproduction Service No. ED 336832)

Hardin, H. (1989). *The privatization putsch.* Halifax, NS: The Institute for Research on Public Policy.

Hargreaves, D. H. (1994). The new professionalism: The synthesis of professional and institutional development. *Teaching & Teacher Education 10*(4), 423–438.

Harlow, J. G. (1962). Purpose-defining: The central function of the school administrator. In J. A. Culbertson & S. P. Hencley (Eds.), *Preparing administrators: New perspectives* (pp. 61–71). Columbus, OH: University Council for Educational Administration.

Harrison, J. W., & Lembeck, E. (1996). Emergent teacher leaders. In G. Moller & M. Katzenmeyer (Eds.), *Every teacher as a leader: Realizing the potential of teacher leadership* (pp. 101–116). San Francisco: Jossey-Bass.

Hart, A. W. (1995). Reconceiving school leadership: Emergent view. *The Elementary School Journal 96*(1), 9–28.

Hart, A. W., & Pounder, P. G. (1999). Reinventing preparation programs: A decade of activity. In J. Murphy & P. B. Forsyth (Eds.), *Educational administration: A decade of reform* (pp. 115–151). Thousand Oaks, CA: Corwin Press.

Harvey, G., & Crandall, D. P. (1988). A beginning look at the what and how of restructuring. In C. Jenks (Ed.), *The redesign of education: A collection of papers concerned with comprehensive educational reform* (pp. 1–37). San Francisco: Far West Laboratory.

Hawley, W. D. (1988). Universities and the improvement of school management. In D. E. Griffiths, R. T. Stout, & P. B. Forsyth (Eds.), *Leaders for America's schools: The report and papers of the National Commission on Excellence in Educational Administration* (pp. 82–88). Berkeley, CA: McCutchan.

Hawley, W. D. (1995). The false premises and false promises of the movement to privatize public education. *Teachers College Record 96*(4), 735–742.

Heifetz, R. A., & Laurie, D. L. (1997, January–February). The work of leadership. *Harvard Business Review 75*(1), 124–135.

Hill, P. T. (1994). Public schools by contract: An alternative to privatization. In S. Hakim, P. Seidenstat, & G. W. Bowman (eds.), Privatizing education and educational choice: Concepts, plans, and experiences (pp. 75–87). Westport, CT: Praeger.

Hill, P. T., & Bonan, J. (1991). *Decentralization and accountability in public education.* Santa Monica, CA: Rand.

Hills, J. (1975). The preparation of administrators: Some observations from the "firing line." *Educational Administration Quarterly 11*(3), 1–20.

Himmelstein, J. L. (1983). The new right. In R. C. Liebman and R. Wuthnow (Eds.), *The New Christian Right: Mobilization and legitimization* (pp. 13–30). New York: Aldine.

Hirsch, W. Z. (1991). *Privatizing government services: An economic analysis of contracting out by local governments.* Los Angeles: University of California, Institute of Industrial Relations.

Hodgkinson, C. (1975). Philosophy, politics, and planning: An extended rationale for synthesis. *Educational Administration Quarterly 11*(1), 11–20.

Holmes Group, The. (1986). *Tomorrow's teachers: A report of the Holmes group.* East Lansing, MI: Author.

Hood, C. (1994). *Explaining economic policy reversals.* Buckingham, England: Open University Press.

Houston, H. M. (1989, March). *Professional development for restructuring: Analysis and recommendations.* Paper presented at the annual meeting of the American Educational Research Association, San Francisco.

Howey, K. R. (1988). Why teacher leadership? *Journal of Teacher Education 39*(1), 28–31.

Immegart, G. L. (1977). The study of educational administration, 1954–1974. In L. L. Cunningham, W. G. Hack, & R. O. Nystrand (Eds.), *Educational administration: The developing decades* (pp. 298–328). Berkeley, CA: McCutchan.

Immegart, G. L. (1990). What is truly missing in advanced preparation in educational administration? *Journal of Educational Administration 28*(3), 5–13.

Jackson, B. L., & Kelley, C. (2002). Educational and innovative programs in educational leadership. *Educational Administration Quarterly 38*(2), 192–212.

Jacobson, S. L. (1990). Reflections on the third wave of reform: Rethinking administrator preparation. In S. L. Jacobson & J. A. Conway (Eds.), *Educational leadership in an age of reform* (pp. 30–44). New York: Longman.

Johnson, S. M. (1989). Schoolwork and its reform. In J. Hannaway & R. Crowson (Eds.), *The politics of reforming school administration* (1989 Yearbook of the Politics of Education Association, pp. 95–112). New York: Falmer.

Katz, M. B. (1971). From volunteerism to bureaucracy in American education. *Sociology of Education 44*(3), 297–332.

Katzenmeyer, M., & Moller, G. (2001). *Awakening the sleeping giant: Helping teachers develop as leaders.* Newbury Park, CA: Corwin Press.

Keedy, J. L. (1999). Examining teacher instructional leadership within the small group dynamics of collegial groups. *Teaching and Teacher Education 15*(7), 785–799.

Killion, J. P. (1996). Moving beyond the school: Teacher leaders in the district office. In G. Moller & M. Katzenmeyer (Eds.), *Every teacher as leader: Realizing the potential of teacher leadership* (pp. 63–84). San Francisco: Jossey-Bass.

Kochan, F., & Twale, K. (1998). Advisory groups in educational leadership: Seeking a bridge between town and gown. *Journal of School Leadership 29*(4), 237–250.

Krug, E. A. (1964). *The shaping of the American high school.* New York: Harper & Row.

Lakomski, G. (1998, Fall). Training administrators in the wild: A naturalistic perspective. *UCEA Review 34*(3), 1, 5, 10–11.

Lambert, L. (2003). *Leadership capacity for lasting school improvement.* Alexandria, VA: Association of Supervision and Curriculum Development.

Lawton, S. B. (1991, September). *Why restructure?* Revision of paper presented at the annual meeting of the American Educational Research Association, Chicago, IL.

Lewis, D. A. (1993). Deinstitutionalization and school decentralization: Making the same mistake twice. In J. Hannaway & M. Carnoy (Eds.), *Decentralization and school improvement* (pp. 84–101). San Francisco: Jossey-Bass.

Lieberman, A., & Miller, L. (1999). *Teachers—transforming their world and their work.* New York: Teachers College Press.

Lieberman, A., Saxl, E. R., & Miles, M. B. (1998). Teacher leadership: Ideology and practice. In A. Lieberman (Ed.), *Building a professional culture in schools* (pp. 148–166). New York: Teachers College Press

Liebman, R. C. (1983a). Introduction. In R. C. Liebman & R. Wuthnow (Eds.), *The new Christian right: Mobilization and legitimization* (pp. 1–9). New York: Aldine.

Liebman, R. C. (1983b). The making of the new Christian right. In R. C. Liebman & R. Wuthnow (Eds.), *The new Christian right: Mobilization and legitimization* (pp. 227–238). New York: Aldine.

Liebman, R. C., & Wuthnow, R. (Eds.) (1983). *The new Christian right: Mobilization and legitimization.* New York: Aldine.

Lindelow, J. (1981). School-based management. In S. C. Smith, J. A. Mazzarella, & P. K. Piele (Eds.), *School leadership: Handbook for survival* (pp. 94–129). Eugene: University of Oregon. (ERIC Clearing House on Educational Management)

Lipham, J. M. (1964). Organizational character of education: Administrative behavior. *Review of Educational Research 34*(4), 435–454.

Little, J. W. (1987). Teachers as colleagues. In V. Richardson-Koehler (Ed.), *Educators' handbook: A research perspective* (pp. 491–518). White Plains, NY: Longman.

Little, J. W., & McLaughlin, M. W. (Eds.). (1993a). Conclusion. In J. W. Little & M. W. McLaughlin. *Teachers work: Individuals, colleagues, and contexts.* New York: Teachers College Press.

Little, J. W., & McLaughlin, M. W. (Eds.). (1993b). Introduction. Perspectives on cultures and contexts of teaching. In J. W. Little & M. W. McLaughlin. *Teachers work: Individuals, colleagues, and contexts* (pp. 1–8). New York: Teachers College Press.

Livingston, C. (1992). *Teachers as leaders: Evolving roles.* Washington, DC: National Education Association.

Lortie, D. (1975). *School teacher.* Chicago: University of Chicago Press.

Louis, K. S., & Miles, M. B. (1990). *Improving the urban high school: What works and why.* New York: Teachers College Press.

Louis, K. S., & Murphy, J. (1994). The evolving role of the principal: Some concluding thoughts. In J. Murphy & K. S. Louis (Eds.), *Reshaping the principalship: Insights from transformational reform efforts* (pp. 265–281). Newbury Park, CA: Corwin Press.

Lynch, M., & Strodl, P. (1991, February). *Teacher leadership: Preliminary development of a questionnaire.* Paper presented at the annual conference of the Eastern Educational Research Association, Boston.

Maccoby, M. (1989, December). *Looking for leadership now.* Paper presented at the National Center for Educational Leadership Conference, Harvard University, Cambridge, MA.

Mann, D. (1975). What peculiarities in educational administration make it difficult to profess: An essay. *Journal of Educational Administration 13*(1), 139–147.

Marks, H. M., & Printy, S. M. (2003). Principal leadership and school performance: An integration of transformational and instructional leadership. *Educational Administration Quarterly 39*(3), 370–397.

Marland, S. P. (1960). Superintendents' concerns about research applications in educational administration. In R. F. Campbell & J. M. Lipham (Eds.), *Administrative theory as a guide to action* (pp. 21–36). Chicago: University of Chicago, Midwest Administration Center.

Marshall, R., & Tucker, M. (1992). *Thinking for a living: Work, skills, and the future of the American economy.* New York: Basic Books.

Martin, B. (1993). *In the public interest? Privatization and public sector reform.* London: Zed Books.

Martin, B., & Crossland, B. J. (2000, October). *The relationships between teacher empowerment, teachers' sense of responsibility for student outcomes and student achievement.* Paper presented at the annual meeting of the Mid-Western Education Research Association, Chicago.

Mayberry, M. (1991, April). *Conflict and social determinism: The reprivatization of education.* Paper presented at the annual meeting of the American Educational Research Association, Chicago, IL.

McCarthy, M. M. (1999). The evolution of educational leadership preparation programs. In J. Murphy & K. S. Louis (Eds.), *Handbook of research on educational administration* (2nd ed., pp. 119–139). San Francisco, Jossey-Bass.

McCarthy, M. M., & Kuh, G. D. (1997). *Continuity and change: The educational leadership professoriate.* Columbia, MO: The University Council for Educational Administration.

McCarthy, M. M., Kuh, G. D., Newell, L. J., & Iacona, C. M. (1988). *Under scrutiny: The educational administration professoriate.* Tempe, AZ: University Council for Educational Administration.

McCarthy, S. J., & Peterson, P. L. (1989, March). *Teacher roles: Weaving new patterns in classroom practice and school organization.* Paper presented at the annual meeting of the American Educational Research Association, San Francisco.

McKerrow, K. (1998). Administrative internships: Quality or quantity? *Journal of School Leadership 8*(2), 171–186.

McNamara, J. F. (1978). Practical significance and statistical models. *Educational Administration Quarterly 14*(1), 48–63.

McNeil, L. M. (1998). Contradictions of control, part 1: Administrators and teachers. *Phi Delta Kappan 69*, 333–339.

Miklos, E. (1983). Evolution in administrator preparation programs. *Educational Administration Quarterly 19*(3), 153–177.

Miklos, E. (1988). Administrator selection, career patterns, succession, and socialization. In N. J. Boyan (Ed.), *Handbook of research on educational administration* (pp. 53–76). New York: Longman.

Milstein, M. (1990). Rethinking the clinical aspects of preparation programs: From theory to practice. In S. L. Jacobson & J. A. Conway (Eds.), *Educational leadership in an age of reform* (pp. 119–130). New York: Longman.

Milstein, M. (1996, October). *Clinical aspects of educational administration preparation programs.* Paper prepared for a workshop of the Mississippi professors of educational administration, Jackson, MS. Unpublished manuscript.

Milstein, M., & Associates. (1993). *Changing the way we prepare educational leaders: The Danforth experience.* Newbury Park, CA: Corwin.

Miskel, C. (1988, October). *Research and the preparation of educational administrators.* Paper presented at the annual meeting of the University Council for Educational Administration, Cincinnati.

Miskel, C., & Sandlin, T. (1981). Survey research in educational administration. *Educational Administration Quarterly 17*(4), 1–20.

Mitchell, B, & Cunningham, L. L. (Eds.) (1990). *Educational leadership and changing contexts of families, communities, and schools.* (89th National Society for the Study of Education Yearbook, Part II). Chicago: University of Chicago Press.

Mojkowski, C., & Fleming, D. (1988). *School-site management: Concepts and approaches.* Andover, MA: Regional Laboratory for Educational Improvement of the Northeast and Islands.

Moore, H. A. (1964). The ferment in school administration. In D. E. Griffiths (Ed.), *Behavioral science and educational administration* (63rd NSSE yearbook, Part II, pp. 11–32). Chicago: University of Chicago Press.

Mulkeen, T. A. (1990, September). *Reinventing school leadership* (pp. 105–105) [Working memo prepared for the Reinventing School Leadership Conference]. Cambridge, MA: National Center for Educational Leadership.

Mulkeen, T. A., Cambron-McCabe, N. H., & Anderson, B. J. (Eds.) (1994). *Democratic leadership: The changing context of administrative preparation.* Norwood, NJ: Ablex.

Mulkeen, T. A., & Cooper, B. S. (1989, March). *Implications of preparing school administrators for knowledge-work organizations.* Paper presented at the annual meeting of the American Educational Research Association, San Francisco.

Mulkeen, T. A., & Tetenbaum, T. J. (1990). Teaching and learning in knowledge organizations: Implications for the preparation of school administrators. *Journal of Educational Administration 28*(3), 14–22.

Murnane, R. J., & Levy, F. (1996). *Teaching the new basic skills: Principles for educating children to thrive in a changing economy.* New York: Free Press.

Murphy, J. (1988). Methodological measurement and conceptual problems in the study of administrator instructional leadership. *Educational Evaluation and Policy Analysis 10*(2), 117–139.

Murphy, J. (1990a). Principal instructional leadership. In L. S. Lotto & P. W. Thurston (Eds.), *Advances in educational administration: Changing perspectives on the school.* (Vol. 1, Part B, pp. 163–200). Greenwich, CT: JAI Press.

Murphy, J. (1990b). Preparing school administrators for the 21st century: The reform agenda. In B. Mitchell & L. L. Cunningham (Eds.), *Educational Leadership and changing contexts of families, communities and schools.* (1990 NASSP Yearbook). Chicago: University of Chicago Press.

Murphy, J. (Ed.). (1990c). *The educational reform movement of the 1980s: Perspectives and cases.* Berkeley, CA: McCutchan.

Murphy, J. (1990d, Fall). Restructuring the technical core of preparation programs in educational administration. *UCEA Review 31*(3), 4–5, 10–13.

Murphy, J. (1991a). The effects of the educational reform movement on departments of educational leadership. *Educational Evaluation and Policy Analysis 13*(1), 49–65.

Murphy, J. (1991b). *Restructuring schools: Capturing and assessing the phenomenon.* New York: Teachers College Press.

Murphy, J. (1992). *The landscape of leadership preparation: Reframing the education of school administrators.* Newbury Park, CA: Corwin Press.

Murphy, J. (Ed.). (1993). *Preparing tomorrow's school leaders: Alternative designs.* University Park, PA: University Council for Educational Administration.

Murphy, J. (1996). *The privatization of schooling: Problems and possibilities.* Newbury Park, CA: Corwin Press.

Murphy, J. (1999a). Changes in preparation programs: Perceptions of department chairs. In J. Murphy & P. Forsyth (Eds.), *Educational administration: A decade of reform* (pp. 170–191). Newbury Park, CA: Corwin Press.

Murphy, J. (1999b). The reform of the profession: A self portrait. In J. Murphy & P. Forsyth (Eds.), *Educational administration: A decade of reform* (pp. 39–68). Newbury Park, CA: Corwin Press.

Murphy, J. (1999c). New consumerism: Evolving market dynamics in the institutional dimension of schooling. In J. Murphy & K. S. Louis (Eds.), *Handbook of research on educational administration* (2nd ed., pp. 405–419). San Francisco: Jossey-Bass.

Murphy, J. (1999d). *The quest for a center: Notes on the state of the profession of educational leadership.* Columbia, MO: University Council for Educational Leadership.

Murphy, J. (2000). Educational governance: The shifting playing field. *Teachers College Record 102*(1), 57–84.

Murphy, J. (2002a). Reculturing the profession of educational leadership: New blueprints. *Educational Administration Quarterly 38*(3), 176–191.

Murphy, J. (Ed.). (2002b). *The educational leadership challenge: Redefining leadership for the 21st century.* (National Society for the Study of Education Yearbook, Vol. 101A). Chicago: University of Chicago Press.

Murphy, J. (2005a). *Connecting teacher leadership and school improvement.* Thousand Oaks, CA: Corwin Press.

Murphy, J. (2005 b). The ISLLC Standards: Exploring the foundations and addressing concerns in the academic community. *Educational Administration Quarterly 41* (1) 154–191.

Murphy, J., & Adams, J. E. (1998). Educational reform in the United States: 1980–2000. *Journal of Educational Administration 36*(5), 426–444.

Murphy, J. & Beck, L. G. (1995). *School-based management as school reform: Taking stock.* Newbury Park: CA: Corwin Press.

Murphy, J., & Datnow, A. (Ed.). (2003). *Leadership for school reform: Lessons from comprehensive reform designs.* Thousand Oaks, CA: Corwin Press.

Murphy, J., & Forsyth, P. (Eds.). (1999). *Educational administration: A decade of reform.* Newbury Park, CA: Corwin Press.

Murphy, J., Gilmer, S., Weise, R., & Page, A. (1998). *Pathways to privatization in education.* Norwood, NJ: Ablex.

Murphy, J., & Hallinger, P. (1986). The superintendent as instructional leader: Findings from effective school districts. *Journal of Educational Administration 24*(2), 213–236.

Murphy, J., Hallinger, P., Lotto, L. S., & Miller, S. K. (1987). Barriers to implementing the instructional leadership role. *Canadian Administrator 27*(3), 1–9.

Murphy, J., Hallinger, P., & Mesa, R. P. (1985). School effectiveness: Checking progress and assumptions and developing a role for state and federal government. *Teachers College Record 86*(4), 615–641.

Murphy, J., & Hawley, W. (2003). The AASA "Leadership for Learning" masters program. *Teaching in Educational Administration 10*(2), 1–6.

Murphy, J., & Louis, K. S. (Eds.). (1999). *Handbook on research on educational administration* (2nd ed.). San Francisco: Jossey-Bass.

Murphy, J., & Shiffman, C. (2002). *Understanding and assessing charter schools.* New York: Teachers College Press.

Murphy, J., & Shipman, N. J. (1999). The Interstate School Leaders Licensure Consortium: A standards based approach to strengthening educational leadership. *Journal of Personnel Evaluation in Education 13*(3), 205–224.

Murphy, J., & Vriesenga, M. (2004). *Research on preparation programs in educational administration: An analysis.* Columbia, MO: University Council for Educational Administration.

Murphy, J., Yff, I., & Shipman, N. J. (2000). Implementation of the Interstate School Leaders Licensure Consortium standards. *The International Journal of Leadership in Education 3*(1), 17–39.

Muth, R. (1989, October). *Reconceptualizing training for educational administrators and leaders: Focus on inquiry* (Notes on Reform, no. 2). Charlottesville, VA: National Policy Board for Educational Administration.

National Commission for the Principalship. (1993). *Principals for our changing schools: Preparation and certification.* Fairfax, VA: Author.

National Commission on Excellence in Educational Administration. (1987). *Leaders for America's schools.* Tempe, AZ: University Council for Educational Administration.

National Commission on Teaching and America's Future. (1996). *What matters most: Teaching for America's future.* New York: Author.

Newlon, J. H. (1934). *Educational administration as social policy.* New York: Scribner.

Newmann, F. M., & Wehlage, G. G. (1995). *Successful school restructuring.* Madison: University of Wisconsin-Madison, Center of Organization and Restructuring of Schools.

Norton, M. S., & Levan, F. D. (1987). Doctoral studies of students in educational administration programs in UCEA member institutions. *Educational Considerations 14*(1), 21–24.

Ogawa, R. T., & Bossert, S. T. (1995). Leadership as an organizational quality. *Educational Administration Quarterly 31*(2), 224–243.

Ogawa, R. T., Goldring, E. B., & Conley, S. (2000). Organizing the field to improve research on educational administration. *Educational Administration Quarterly 36*(3), 340–357.

Olson, L. (1992). A matter of choice: Minnesota puts "charter schools" idea to test. *Education Week 12*(1), 10–11.

Orr, T., & Kottkamp, R. (2003, April). *Evaluating the causal pathway from leadership preparation to school improvement.* Paper presented at the annual meeting of the American Educational Research Association, Chicago.

Osin, L., & Lesgold, A. (1996, Winter). A proposal for the reengineering of the educational system. *Review of Educational Research 66*(4), 621–656.

Pellicer, L. O., & Anderson, L. W. (1995). *A handbook for teacher leaders.* Thousand Oaks, Corwin Press.

Peterson, K. D., & Finn, C. E. (1985). Principals, superintendents and the administrator's art. *The Public Interest 79*, 42–62.

Petrie, H. G. (1990). Reflecting on the second wave of reform: Restructuring the teaching profession. In S. L. Jacobson & J. A. Conway (Eds.), *Educational leadership in an age of reform* (pp. 14–29). New York: Longman.

Popper, S. H. (1982). An advocate's case for the humanities in preparation programs for school administration. *Journal of Educational Administration 20*(1), 12–22.

Pounder, D. G. (2000). A discussion of the task force's collective findings. *Educational Administration Quarterly 36*(3), 465–473.

Pounder, D. G., Ogawa, R. T., & Adams, E. A. (1995). Leadership as an organization-wide phenomena: Its impact on school performance. *Educational Administration Quarterly 31*(4), 564–588.

Powell, A. G., Farrar, E., & Cohen, D. K. (1985). *The shopping mall high school: Winners and losers in the educational marketplace.* Boston: Houghton-Mifflin.

Prawat, R. S., & Peterson, P. L. (1999). Social constructivist views of learning. In J. Murphy & K. S. Louis (Eds.), *Handbook of research on educational administration* (2nd ed., pp. 203–226). San Francisco: Jossey-Bass.

President's Commission on Privatization. (1988). *Privatization: Toward a more effective government.* Washington, DC: U.S. Government.

Prestine, N. A. (1995). Crisscrossing the landscape: Another turn at cognition and educational administration. *Educational Administration Quarterly 31*(1), 134–142.

Purkey, S. D., & Smith, M. S. (1983). Effective schools: A review. *Elementary School Journal 83*(4), 427–452.

Putnam, R. D. (1995). Bowling alone: America's declining social capital. *Journal of Democracy 6*(1), 65–77.

Rallis, S. F. (1990). Professional teachers and restructured schools: Leadership challenges. In B. Mitchell & L. L. Cunningham (Eds.), *Educational leadership and changing contexts of families, communities, and schools* (89th NSSE Yearbook, Part II, pp. 184–209). Chicago: University of Chicago Press.

Retallick, J., & Fink, D. (2002). Framing leadership: Contributions and impediments to educational change. *International Journal of Leadership in Education 5*(2), 91–104.

Reyes, P., Wagstaff, L. H., & Fusarelli, L. D. (1999). Delta forces: The changing fabric of American society and education. In J. Murphy & K. S. Louis (Eds.), *Handbook of research on educational administration* (2nd ed., pp. 183–201). San Francisco: Jossey-Bass.

Riehl, C., Larson, C. L., Short, P. M., & Reitzug, U. C. (2000). Reconceptualizing research and scholarship in educational administration: Learning to know, knowing to do, and doing to learn. *Educational Administration Quarterly* 36(3), 391–427.

Rosenholtz, S. J. (1989). *Teachers' workplace: The social organization of schools.* White Plains, NY: Longman.

Ross, R. L. (1988). *Government and the private sector: Who should do what?* New York: Crane Russak.

Rowan, B. (1995). Research on learning and teaching in K–12 school: Implications for the field of educational administration. *Educational Administration Quarterly 31*(1), 115–133.

Rowe, K. J. (1995). Factors affecting students' progress in reading: Key findings from a longitudinal study. *Literacy, Teaching and Learning 1*(2), 57–110.

Rungeling, B., & Glover, R. W. (1991). Educational restructuring—the process for change? *Urban Education 25*(4), 415–427.

Rusch, E. (2004, Fall). Social justice work: From intellectualizing to practice. *UCEA Review 43*(3), 12–14.

Sackney, L. E., & Dibski, D. J. (1992, August). *School-based management: A critical perspective.* Paper presented at the Seventh Regional Conference of the Commonwealth Council for Educational Administration, Hong Kong.

Sarason, S. B. (1994). *Parental involvement and the political principle: Why the existing governance structure of schools should be abolished.* San Francisco: Jossey-Bass.

Schlechty, P. C. (1990). *Schools for the 21st century: Leadership imperatives for educational reform.* San Francisco: Jossey-Bass.

Seeley, D. S. (1988). A new vision for public education. *Youth Policy 10*(2), 34–36.

Sergiovanni, T. J. (1984). Developing a relevant theory of administration. In T. J. Sergiovanni, & J. E. Corbally (Eds.), *Leadership and organizational culture: New perspectives on administrative theory and practice* (pp. 275–291). Urbana: University of Illinois Press.

Sergiovanni, T. J. (1989). Mystics, neats, and scruffies: Informing professional practice in educational administration. *The Journal of Educational Administration 27*(2), 7–21.

Sergiovanni, T. J. (1990). *Value-added leadership: How to get extraordinary performance in schools.* San Diego: Harcourt, Brace, & Jovanovich.

Sergiovanni, T. J. (1991). *The principalship: A reflective practice perspective* (2nd ed.). Boston: Allyn & Bacon.

Sergiovanni, T. J. (1992). Why we should seek substitutes for leadership. *Leadership 49*(5), 41–45.

Sergiovanni, T. J. (1994). Organizations or communities? Changing the metaphor changes the theory. *Educational Administration Quarterly 30*(2), 214–226.

Shakeshaft, C. (1988). Women in educational administration: Implications for training. In D. E. Griffiths, R. T. Stout, & P. R. Forsyth (Eds.), *Leaders for tomorrow's schools* (pp. 403–416). Berkeley, CA: McCutchan.

Shakeshaft, C. (1999). The struggle to create a more gender-inclusive profession. In J. Murphy & K. S. Louis (Eds.), *Handbook of research on educational administration* (2nd ed., pp. 99–118). San Francisco: Jossey-Bass.

Silva, D. Y., Gimbert, B., & Nolan, J. (2000). Sliding the doors: Locking and unlocking possibilities for teacher leadership. *Teachers College Record 102*(4), 779–804.

Silver, P. F. (1978a). Some areas of concern in administrator preparation. In P. F. Silver & D. W. Spuck (Eds.), *Preparatory programs for educational administrators in the United States* (pp. 202–215). Columbus, OH: University Council for Educational Administration.

Silver, P. F. (1978b). Trends in program development. In P. F. Silver & D. W. Spuck (Eds.), *Preparatory programs for educational administrators in the United States* (pp. 178–201). Columbus, OH: University Council for Educational Administration.

Silver, P. F. (1982). Administrator preparation. In H. E. Mitzel (Ed.), *Encyclopedia of educational research* (5th ed., Vol. 1, pp. 49–59). New York: Free Press.

Silver, P. F., & Spuck, D. W. (Eds.). (1978). *Preparatory programs for educational administrators in the United States.* Columbus, OH: University Council for Educational Administration.

Sizer, T. R. (1984). *Horace's compromise: The dilemma of the American high school.* Boston: Houghton-Mifflin.

Smylie, M. A. (1995). New perspectives on teacher leadership. *The Elementary School Journal, 96*(1), 3–7.

Smylie, M. A., Conley, S., & Marks, H. M. (2002). Exploring new approaches to teacher leadership for school improvement. In J. Murphy (Ed.), *The educational leadership challenge: Redefining leadership for the 21st century* (101st yearbook of the National Society for the Study of Education, Part I, pp. 162–188). Chicago: University of Chicago Press.

Smylie, M. A., & Hart, A. W. (1999). School leadership for teacher learning: A human and social capital development perspective. In J. Murphy & K. S. Louis, *Handbook of research on educational administration* (2nd ed., pp. 421–441). San Francisco: Jossey-Bass.

Smylie, M. A., Wenzel, S. A., & Fendt, C. R. (2003). The Chicago Annenberg Challenge: Lessons on leadership for school development. In J. Murphy & A.

Datnow (Eds.), *Leadership for school reform: Lessons from comprehensive school reforms* (pp. 135–158). Thousand Oaks, CA: Corwin Press.

Snauwaert, D. T. (1993). *Democracy, education, and governance: A developmental conception.* Albany: State University of New York Press.

Snow, C. E., Burns, M. S., & Griffin, P. (Eds.) (1998). *Preventing reading difficulties in young children.* Washington, DC: National Academy Press.

Spillane, J. P., Diamond, J. B., & Jita, L. (2000, April). *Leading classroom instruction. A preliminary explanation of the distribution of leading practice.* Paper presented at the annual meeting of the American Educational Research Association, New Orleans.

Spillane, J. P., Halverson, R., & Diamond, J. B. (n.d.). *Toward a theory of leadership practice: A distributed perspective.* Evanston, IL: Institute for Policy Research, Northwestern University.

Starr, P. (1991). The case for skepticism. In W. T. Gormley (Ed.), *Privatization and its alternatives* (pp. 25–36). Madison: The University of Wisconsin Press.

Stigler, J. W., & Hiebert, J. (1999). *The teaching gap: Best ideas from the world's teachers for improving education in the classroom.* New York: Free Press.

Stone, M., Horejs, J., & Lomas, A. (1997). Commonalities and differences in teacher leadership at the elementary, middle, and high school level. *Action in Teacher Education 19*(3), 49–64.

Sykes, G. (1999). The "new professionalism" in education: An appraisal. In J. Murphy & K. S. Louis (Eds.), *Handbook of research on educational administration* (2nd ed., pp. 227–249). San Francisco: Jossey-Bass.

Sykes, G., & Elmore, R. F. (1989). Making schools more manageable. In J. Hannaway & R. L. Crowson (Eds.), *The politics of reforming school administrations* (pp. 77–94). New York: Falmer Press.

Teddlie, C., & Reynolds, D. (2000). *The international handbook of school effectiveness research.* London: Falmer.

Thayer, F. C. (1987). Privatization: Carnage, chaos, and corruption. In B. J. Carroll, R. W. Conant, & T. A. Easton (Eds.), *Private means, public ends: Private business in social service delivery* (pp. 146–170). New York: Praeger.

Thurpp, M. (2003). The school leadership literature in managerealist times: Exploring the problem of textual apologism. *School Leadership & Management 23*(2), 149–172.

Tomlinson, J. (1986). Public education, public good. *Oxford Review of Education 12*(3), 211–222.

Tschannen-Moran, M., Firestone, W. A., Hoy, W. K., & Johnson, S. M. (2000). The write stuff: A study of productive scholars in educational administration. *Educational Administration Quarterly 36*(3), 358–390.

Tyack, D. B. (1993). School governance in the United States: Historical puzzles and anomalies. In J. Hannaway & M. Carnoy (Eds.), *Decentralization and school improvement* (pp. 1–32). San Francisco: Jossey-Bass.

Tyack, D. B., & Cummings, R. (1977). Leadership in American public schools before 1954: Historical configurations and conjectures. In L. L. Cunningham, W. G. Hack, & R. O. Nystrand (Eds.), *Educational administration: The developing decades* (pp. 46–66). Berkeley, CA: McCutchan.

Tyack, D. B., & Hansot, E. (1982). *Managers of virtue: Public school leadership in America, 1920–1980.* New York: Basic Books.

Uline, C. L., & Berkowitz, J. M. (2000). Transforming school culture through teaching teams. *Journal of School Leadership 10*(1), 416–444.

Wasley, P. A. (1991). *Teachers who lead: The rhetoric of reform and realities of practice.* New York: Teachers College Press.

Watkins, J. M., & Lusi, S. F. (1989). *Facing the essential tensions: Restructuring from where you are.* Paper presented at the annual meeting of the American Educational Research Association, San Francisco.

Weick, K. E., & McDaniel, R. R. (1989). How professional organizations work: Implications for school organization and management. In T. J. Sergiovanni & J. H. Moore (Eds.), *Schooling for tomorrow: Directing reforms to issues that count* (pp. 330–355). Boston: Allyn & Bacon.

Wellisch, J. B., MacQueen, A. H., Carriere, R. A., & Duck, G. A. (1978). School management and organization in successful schools. *Sociology of Education 51*, 211–226.

Whitty, G. (1984). The privatization of education. *Educational Leadership 41*(7), 51–54.

Willower, D. J. (1983). Evolutions in the professorship: Past philosophy, future. *Educational Administration Quarterly 19*(3), 179–200.

Willower, D. J. (1988). Synthesis and projection. In N. J. Boyan (Ed.), *Handbook of research on educational administration* (pp. 729–747). New York: Longman.

Wilson, S. M., Flodenz, R. E., & Ferrini-Mundy, J. (2001). *Teacher preparation research: Current knowledge, gaps, and recommendations.* Seattle: Center for the Study of Teaching and Policy, University of Washington.

Wise, A. E. (1978). The hyper-rationalization of American education. *Educational Leadership 35*(5), 354–361.

Wise, A. E. (1989). Professional teaching: A new paradigm for the management of education. In T. J. Sergiovanni & J. H. Moore (Eds.), *Schooling for tomorrow: Directing reforms to issues that count* (pp. 301–310). Boston: Allyn & Bacon.

Wynn, R. (1957). Organization and administration of the professional program. In R. F. Campbell & R. T. Gregg (Eds.), *Administrative behavior in education* (pp. 464–509). New York: Harper.

Young, M. D., & Peterson, G. J. (2002). The National Commission for the Advancement of Educational Leadership Preparation: An introduction. *Educational Administration Quarterly 38*(2), 130–136.

Index

About the Commentors

Martha McCarthy is a Chancellor's Professor at Indiana University and directs the High School Survey of Student Engagement. She received her Ph.D. from the University of Florida, and she specializes in education law and policy. Previously chair of the Educational Leadership Program and director of the Indiana Education Policy Center, she has also been a public school teacher and administrator. She has authored or coauthored nine books and more than 200 articles on students' and teachers' rights, church-state relations, equity issues, school privatization, leadership preparation programs, and high school student engagement. She has served as president of the Education Law Association and the University Council for Educational Administration and vice-president for Division A of the American Educational Research Association. Among recent awards, she has received the Living Legend Award from the National Council of Professors of Educational Administration (2002), the Sylvia Bowman Award for Exemplary Teaching from the Indiana University System (2004), and the Roald Campbell Lifetime Achievement Award from UCEA (2004).

Gary L. Anderson is a professor in the Department of Administration, Leadership, and Technology at the Steinhardt School of Education, New York University. His current research focuses on the impact of neoliberal economic policies on schools and communities. Recent books include *Performance Theories in Education: Power, Pedagogy* and *The Politics of*

Identity (2005), and *The Action Research Dissertation: A Guide for Students and Faculty* (2005).

Diana Pounder is professor and chair of the Department of Educational Leadership and Policy at the University of Utah-Salt Lake City, and current Editor of *Educational Administration Quarterly (EAQ)*. Dr. Pounder has been active and assumed leadership roles in national professional organizations, including past president of the University Council for Educational Administration (UCEA), and past secretary of Division A of the American Educational Research Association (AERA). She participates actively in a variety of state and national education and policy initiatives, the most recent of which have focused largely on improving and assessing school leadership preparation. Dr. Pounder's scholarly publications appear in *Educational Administration Quarterly, Journal of School Leadership, The Australian Journal of Education, Educational Leadership, The School Administrator*, and other prominent publication outlets. These works include largely empirical research on school leader preparation effectiveness, professor and principal shortages and job desirability, teacher work-group effectiveness, distributed leadership, equity in personnel selection and compensation, and other interests related to attracting, retaining, motivating, and developing professional educators. Her research awards include the 1996 Davis Award for Outstanding *EAQ* article (coauthored with Rod Ogawa and Ann Adams), and both the Department of Educational Leadership research award and the College of Education research award from the University of Utah.

Gary M. Crow is a professor in the Department of Educational Leadership and Policy at The University of Utah (USA). He received his Ph.D. degree in educational administration from the University of Chicago. His research interests include work socialization of school site leaders, the principalship, leadership, and school reform. He is currently conducting comparative studies of the socialization of U.K. head teachers and U.S. principals. His most recent book is *Being and Becoming a Principal* (with J. Matthews, Allyn and Bacon) and his articles have appeared in *Educational Management and Administration* (UK), *Educational Administration Quarterly, Journal of School Leadership, Journal of Educational Administration*, and *Urban Education*. He is currently president of the University Council for Educational Administration.

Michelle D. Young is the executive director of the University Council for Educational Administration (UCEA) and a faculty member in the Department of Educational Leadership and Policy Analysis at the University of Missouri-Columbia. UCEA is an international consortium of research institutions with doctoral programs in educational leadership and administration. In her role as executive director of UCEA, Young works with universities, practitioners, professional organizations, and state and national leaders to continually improve the preparation and practice of school and school system leaders and to create a dynamic base of knowledge on excellence in educational leadership. Young routinely works with states and universities on program improvement projects and serves on a number of national boards that focus on increasing knowledge of and improving practice in educational leadership. Young serves on the Wallace Foundation's Education Advisory Committee, the Institute for Educational Leadership's E-Lead Advisory Board, the National Policy Board for Educational Administration, and the National Commission for the Advancement of Educational Leadership Preparation. She also served on the National Advisory Board for ERIC through December 2003. Young received her Ph.D. at the University of Texas at Austin in educational policy and planning and then served as an assistant professor in the Department of Policy, Planning, and Leadership Studies at the University of Iowa. Her scholarship focuses on the preparation and practice of school leaders and school policies that facilitate equitable and quality experiences for all students and adults who learn and work in schools. Young is the recipient of the William J. Davis award for the most outstanding article published in a volume of the *Educational Administration Quarterly*. Her work has also been published in the *Review of Educational Research,* the *Educational Researcher*, the *American Educational Research Journal*, the *Journal of School Leadership*, the *International Journal of Qualitative Studies in Education*, and *Leadership and Policy in Schools*, among other publications. She currently serves on the editorial boards of the *Educational Administration Quarterly*, *Educational Administration Abstracts*, and *Education and Urban Society*.

About the Author

Joseph Murphy is associate dean and professor of education at Peabody College of Education of Vanderbilt University. He has also been a faculty member at the University of Illinois and The Ohio State University, where he was the William Ray Flesher Professor of Education. In the public schools, he has served as an administrator at the school, district, and state levels, including an appointment as the executive assistant to the chief deputy superintendent of public instruction in California. His most recent appointment was as the founding president of the Ohio Principals Leadership Academy. At the university level, he has served as department chair and associate dean. He is a past program chair for Division A of AERA and a past vice-president of AERA. He was the founding chair (1994–2004) of the Interstate School Leaders Licensure Consortium (ISLLC) and directed the development of the *ISLLC Standards for School Leaders*. Murphy is the co-editor of the *AERA Handbook of Research on Education Administration* (1999) and editor of the National Society for the Study of Education (NSSE) yearbook *The Educational Leadership Challenge* (2002). His work is in the area of school improvement, with special emphasis on leadership and policy. He has authored or coauthored 14 books and 2 major monographs in this area and edited another 11 books. His most recent authored volumes include *Understanding and Assessing the Charter School Movement* (2002), *Leadership for Literacy* (2004), and *Connecting Teacher Leadership and School Improvement* (2005). He has also published over 200 articles and book chapters on school improvement and leadership.